white heat

25th ANNIVERSARY EDITION

TO MY MOTHER, ALEXANDRA, LETICIA, AND ALBERT

wh

25th ANNIVERSARY EDITION

Marco Pierre White

**PHOTOGRAPHS BY
BOB CARLOS CLARKE**

white heat

FOOD PHOTOGRAPHY BY MICHAEL BOYS

MITCHELL BEAZLEY

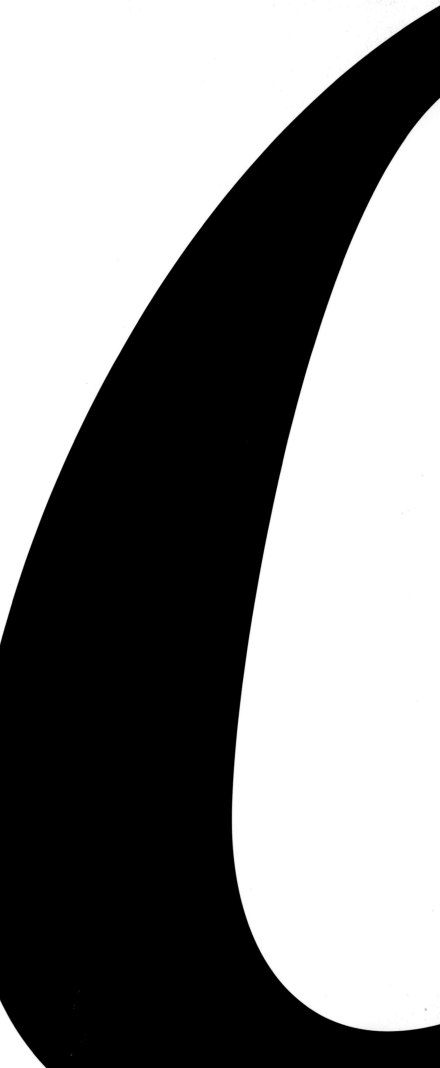

In memory of Bob Carlos Clarke
1950–2006

White Heat
By Marco Pierre White

An Hachette UK Company
www.hachette.co.uk

First published in Great Britain in 1990

This edition published in 2015 by Mitchell Beazley,
a division of Octopus Publishing Group Ltd,
Endeavour House, 189 Shaftesbury Avenue, London WC2H 8JY
www.octopusbooks.co.uk
www.octopusbooksusa.com

Text copyright © Marco Pierre White 1990, 2015
Black and white photographs copyright © The Estate of Bob Carlos Clarke 1990, 2015
Epilogue copyright © James Steen 2015

Distributed in the US by Hachette Book Group
1290 Avenue of the Americas, 4th and 5th Floors, New York, NY 10020

Distributed in Canada by Canadian Manda Group
664 Annette St., Toronto, Ontario, Canada M6S 2C8

Original edition packaged by Amazon Publishing Ltd

ISBN 978-1-78472-000-1

A CIP catalog record for this book is available from the British Library.

Printed and bound in China

10 9 8 7 6 5 4 3 2 1

For the original edition
Design: Clive Hayball and David Rowley of The Image
Editors: Kay Avila, Andrew Jefford
Recipe Editor and Tester: Lewis Esson
Food Photography: Michael Boys

For the 25th anniversary edition
Publishing Director: Stephanie Jackson
Art Director: Jonathan Christie
Design: David Rowley
Production Manager: Peter Hunt
Editorial Assistant: Natalie Bradley

Note
Marco makes his own stocks for use in the recipes (see pages 116 and 117)
but to save time you can use a stock cube instead.

*C*ontents

FOREWORD   6

INTRODUCTION   8

THE HEAT OF THE KITCHEN   16

THE FOOD OF THE GODS

     FIRST COURSES   56

     FISH DISHES   70

     MEAT DISHES   84

     DESSERTS   100

     BASICS   116

EPILOGUE   126

INDEX OF RECIPES AND ACKNOWLEDGMENTS   190

MARCO PIERRE WHITE turned up at Le Gavroche in London at the age of 19 directly from Yorkshire. He had no appointment and only £5 in his pocket. I looked first at the shining eyes as he talked about cooking and then I looked at his long hair. I agreed that he should become an apprentice if he would cut his hair. He did!

Of all the people for whom Marco has worked, I believe that I am the one that knows more about what is inside him. He is not what has been portrayed with relish by the media, at least not the Marco Pierre White that I know. He is one of the kindest and softest people one would ever wish to meet.

As for his cooking it is evident that his genius is reflected on the plate. I do worry that his intensity and his tendency to burn the candle at both ends may burn out his enthusiasm but if he learns to pace himself I know that the sky is the limit for Marco Pierre White and his cooking.

ALBERT H. ROUX

Maître Cuisinier de France

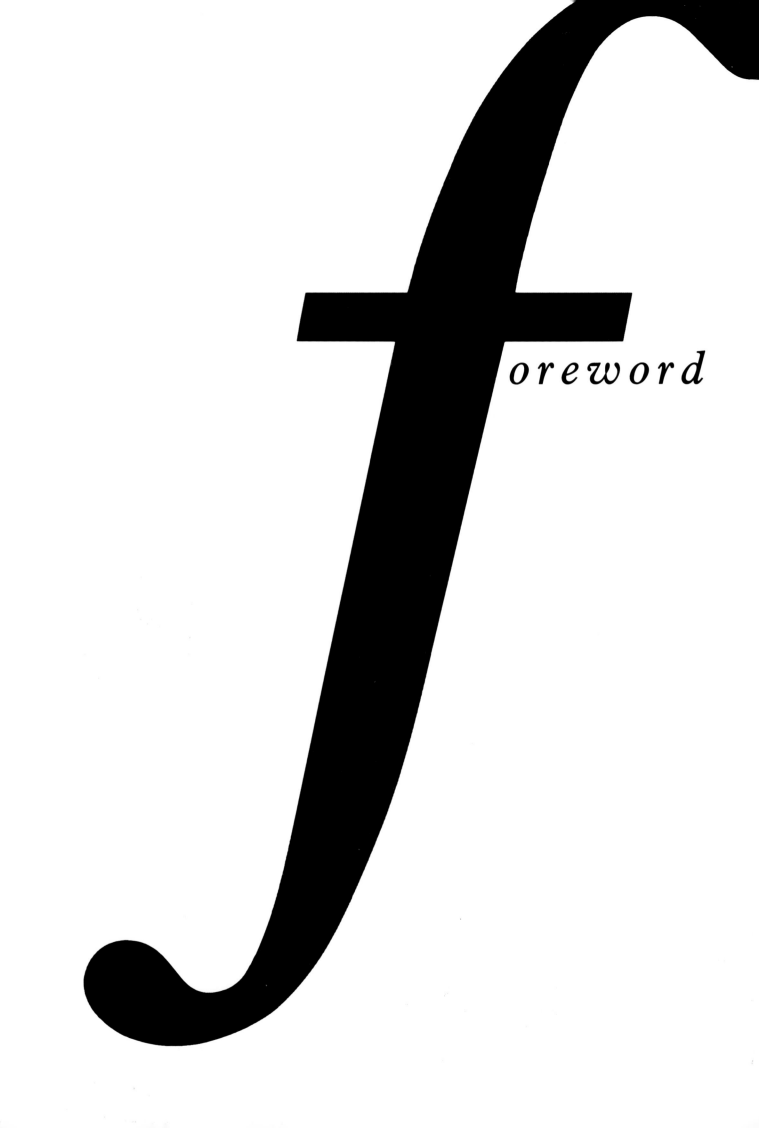

*f*oreword

You're buying *White Heat* because you want to cook well? Because you want to cook Michelin stars? Forget it. Save your money. Go and buy a saucepan.

You want ideas, inspiration, a bit of Marco? Then maybe you'll get something out of this book. I warn you, though, it's a jigsaw, and there's a hundred pieces missing. What do you expect? I'm just at the beginning of my career. You're not going to see the true Marco until I'm 35 or 40. I haven't even been to France yet. But what's here is me, 1990 vintage, built on a foundation of energy and honesty and quality.

I still have a huge amount left to learn. Everything changes in the restaurant, every day. By the time you read this, by the time you start using my ideas, the recipes will have changed. I'm never satisfied with anything I do, never. Almost never. The tagliatelle of oysters, I'm satisfied with that, I can't do anything better with it. Or the pig's foot—but that's Pierre Koffmann's dish, that's his perfection. Everything else I'm still thinking about, I'm still working on. Why do you think I still wear a blue apron?

Marco Pierre, that's Italian and French, and Marco alone is pure Italian. While White—Whitey—he's just a lad from Yorkshire. "Whitey, you'll be nothing in life"— that's what my headmaster said when I left school. He was absolutely right. I've had a lot of publicity, I've got money in my pocket, but what does that mean? You think it makes me somebody? I don't think it does.

My mother was Italian and she died when I was six. I was the third son. Graham, Clive—then Marco. Perhaps with the third son my mother felt she could assert her roots, so she gave me an Italian name. For six years I was my mother's child, the youngest, the little boy. Then came Craig, and two days after giving birth to Craig she died. Craig went off to my aunt in Italy. He's an Italian. I haven't seen him for fifteen years. I don't see any of my brothers or my father much now.

My link with Italy is my dream. That's the only place where I was happy when I was a boy. I used to climb trees to pick peaches and cherries. We ate ravioli almost every day, filled with vegetables. When I make ravioli now I remember all that, being there with Graham and Clive, the cherry trees. Life was easy and warm.

Italy is flair and style. Italian people are expressive, artistic. Whatever position I've held in the kitchen, I've always been an artist. A good kitchen is staffed by artists and donkeys. You need both.

I've been a donkey, too, of course; a grafter. After my mother died, life at home in Yorkshire was very strict and severe, very Victorian. I had to polish my shoes from heel to toe. I was teased at school for my name, for not having a mother, but I was bigger than everyone else. I fought my way through school. My differences

introd

became my strengths in the end. Yorkshire people are very straightforward, blunt. Hardly subtle, are they? I know how to give a good bollocking, and I've taken a few, too. You get Yorkshire portions at Harveys, not London portions.

It has taken me a while to admit where I started cooking, but it was the Hotel St. George in Harrogate, Yorkshire. I was sixteen and I didn't want to be a chef. I simply wanted freedom and a good time.

I began on day one at 7.30 A.M. and I can't remember when I finished. My first job was to strain an enormous stockpot. I was given a chinois and a small ladle. The stock was a thick glutinous gel and it took me three hours to force it through the sieve—no one told me to warm it first and then pour it through. They just left me to it. No one mentioned eating, either. At eight o'clock that night they told me to clean a big walk-in refrigerator and put everything in fresh containers. I was absolutely starving and took a fingerful of something out of one of the basins. In seconds it was all gone. About an hour later a panicking pastrycook raced through the kitchen shouting for his bavarois. I hadn't a clue what a bavarois was. It was only when I found out what it was, maybe a year later, that I realized I'd eaten what he'd been looking for. My main job there was bookie's runner for the head chef. I learned a lot about gambling.

Pierre Koffmann

"Marco only came to steal my recipes. But he's one of the best chefs I ever had in my kitchen – always looking, always listening, wanting to absorb as much as possible as quickly as possible."

uction

"One potage, two fondant, two raviolis, seconds . . . Dress in ten seconds. Simon, start filling up the bass. On my Table one . . . Use your fingers, I don't care if you burn them,

From Harrogate I went all of fifteen miles down the road to the Box Tree at Ilkley. It was here that food began to become an obsession. Michael Lawson was a gentleman's cook. He'd never had a classical training but had dined in all the two- and three-star Michelin restaurants in France and gained his knowledge that way. His food was grand and extravagant: noisettes of lamb topped with foie gras served with a truffle sauce; roast duck with three liqueurs. The Mousseline of Sole Reputation sat like a massive cushion on a julienne of vegetables and truffles; it was classic and superb. Michael really opened the door to cooking for me. I still remember with pride the time I made a sauce and he told me it tasted as good as his. I felt secure in my new-found obsession, and lucky to be a part of the Box Tree. I would sit and clean the copper and the silver after everyone else had gone home. I relished every ritual.

A couple of years later I went for an interview at Chewton Glen in Hampshire and missed the last train home afterward. So I walked around London all night —I only had £7.36 on me. The next morning I called at Gavroche. I'd applied to work there earlier, but the application form was in French and I couldn't understand it. I talked to Albert Roux, and he gave me a job.

I knew a lot about food by then, but it was still like starting over. The methods were different and the repertoire was colossal. But the food inspired me,

and so did Albert. You can't separate a great cook from his dishes. I was inspired by the honesty, the attention to detail, the controlled extravagance that I found at Gavroche. Albert taught me the proper use of extra-vagance, and he was one of the few people who could control me. He's been like a father figure to me over the years. He had time for me and tried to understand me and I thank him for that.

I went to Nico next. In fact I went to Nico for £50 in the mornings and Gavroche in the afternoons and evenings. I didn't stop still, I didn't have time for sleep or social life or anything else except cooking, learning, working, thinking. I still don't.

Nico is the true gourmet. I've never met anyone who had as much appreciation of food as Nico does. He loves eating. If he hadn't been a great chef he would have been the most knowledgeable and respected food journalist. But he's also a great technician, and he runs one of the most consistent restaurants in the UK. I suppose I learned about the slow pursuit of perfection from Nico, the constant quest to lift everything one notch higher the whole time. He's exactly double my age, he's moved his restaurant five times, and he's still chipping away, refining, never faltering. You need incredible strength and resolve to do that. For me things change all the time, the world is peaks and troughs, everything goes up and down; Nico's up there on a plateau, checking the compass to make sure he's on course.

one pigeon, one lamb, one veal . . . Hold on one minute . . . Thirty board—come on, dress dress dress . . . Let me salt it . . .What table is this? you weren't given fingers not to burn them. Quickly quickly quickly . . ."

Service at Harvey's

I suppose I got to some kind of a peak when I was working for Nico, then I hit a trough. I gave up my job and went on a big bender, became a gastro-punk. From time to time I'd cook casually, make enough money to last a few more weeks, then I'd blow off again. It was great to be decadent. At first, anyway. But eventually I couldn't stand watching another person getting drunk or someone else injecting smack into their veins. Eighteen months and I'd had enough of the world outside. I needed to get back into the kitchen. But in cookery terms, I'd cooked my goose.

Pierre Koffmann started me on my rehabilitation course. I turned up out of the blue one morning and asked if I could work in his kitchen for a day—without pay. I turned up again the next day, and the next, and every day for a month, until finally one of his team left and he was able to offer me a paid place in his kitchen.

I had to prove myself all over again, completely. He saw that I was prepared to stand outside cleaning scallops in the cold. He saw I could scoop quenelles in one. Eventually I was included in the chefs' teatime, and then I knew that I'd earned his respect. It took time, though. Unlike me, Pierre doesn't talk when he works—his is a silent kitchen. He expresses himself in his food. You see Pierre on every plate. He serves what he likes eating, not what he thinks will earn him Michelin stars. His cooking seems effortless, and in many ways I think it is. It comes naturally, from his heritage, the cookery of Southwest France.

I learned about bread from Pierre. He has a passion for bread. Serve good bread and butter before the meal and all will be well. Also a few lessons in humility—not my strong point, I know. Pierre has shunned publicity all his life. Perhaps one day I'll be at one with myself, as he is. Maybe in Italy. Who knows?

Before I went to work for Raymond Blanc at the Manoir aux Quat' Saisons I had to promise Nico I'd stay there a year. So I did. I needed the credibility.

Raymond couldn't hold the reins on me, though. I was in a hurry, and too talented for my age. He knew I had flair—and I knew I had flair. I can throw something on a plate and it will look wonderful, but it was with Raymond that I developed my sense of taste. He's incredibly talented in that way. Food should taste of what it is—that's common sense, of course, but few people actually realize it. Raymond does. He has an extraordinary sense of taste.

Of all the chefs I worked for, I know that I'm most similar to Raymond. There's an element of madness in us both. It's only a matter of time before the asylum catches up with me or with Raymond. I think they'll catch him first because he can't run as fast as I can. Perhaps they'll get us both in the end. Then we won't be in chef's jackets; we'll be in straitjackets.

I'm a closing chapter of the eighties—a finale. The decade started with Anton Mosimann, the Roux brothers, Pierre, Nico, and Raymond; they each have their

"The rest of the catering world think I'm on drugs, but that just proves how narrow-minded they all are. If I was on drugs I wouldn't be able to carry on, and I wouldn't have any ideas. I look the way I do because I'm exhausted, because I'm giving everything I've got, but that's the only way I can work and think."

Marco

fledglings coming through now. But I'm an offspring of them all, a hybrid.

The boys in my team know that if they want to get to the top they've got to take the shit. Harveys is the hardest kitchen in Britain; it's the SAS of kitchens. But you don't get to the top by being pampered.

A fish rots from the head, I have to lead from the head; I have to set an example. I have to move twice as fast as everyone else, because I'm the boss.

I wouldn't say I rule with a rod of iron. If someone wants a hard time I'll show them what a hard time is. If someone wants to learn I'll show them how. But if I had a sloppy attitude then I'd be wasting my boy's time. When a boy comes to me he is putting his career in my hands; if he really wants to learn then he'll accept everything that comes his way. He'll leave as a good cook and in a few years he could have his own restaurant with a Michelin star and lead a good life.

Any chef who says he does it for love is a liar. At the end of the day it's all about money. I never thought I would ever think like that but I do now. I don't enjoy it. I don't enjoy having to kill myself six days a week to pay the bank. But if you don't cut the mustard you're finished. If you've got no money you can't do anything; you're a prisoner of society. At the end of the day it's just another job. It's all sweat and toil and dirt: it's misery.

This profession is full of very insecure people backstabbing each other. Rather than spending their time bitching they should be channeling their energies into creating things—that's the only way you get recognition and cred in this world. But ninety percent of the chefs in this country are just laborers. Their brains wouldn't fill a square inch of my kitchen. The catering world in Britain is like the French Foreign Legion; it's the last resort of the inadequate. Anyone who falls out of school falls into catering. You don't need brains to get by, but you do need brains to get to the top. That's why people like Alistair Little, Rowley Leigh, and Simon Hopkinson have gone far—they actually have something to say.

"Marco is a man who is running at a hundred miles an hour. If he doesn't burn himself out – and somehow I think he won't – he'll go right to the top."

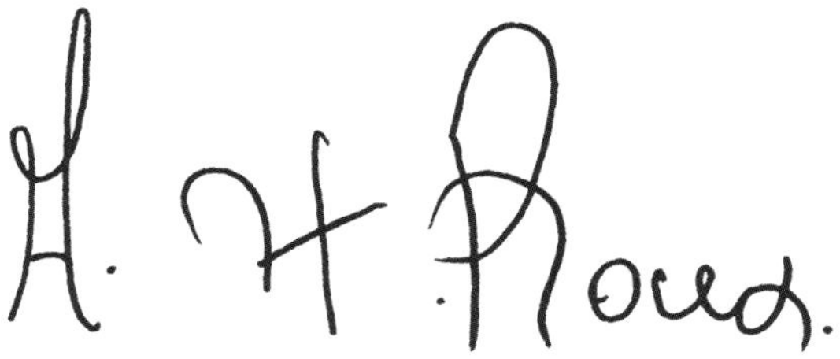

Albert Roux

I wish I wasn't a cook. I wish cooking was just a passionate hobby, but it's an obsession. I caught the bug at the Box Tree and it's terminal. I used to dream about food—smells, tastes, textures. That must be how dishes come to me. All these ideas steam away in my head like old cabbage leaves in a compost heap, and then one day something clicks and they get translated into beautiful food on a plate.

I create things, reject them, and then bring them back again. The nage of sole, for example: I used to love it, then I got fed up with it, and it's only now that Michael Boys has captured it for this book that I realize what a good dish it really is.

There's only one dish on my menu that is perfect, and that's the tagliatelle of oysters with caviar. It's pure theatre to make, and it's pure theatre to eat. It's so sensuous that everyone who eats it wants another portion. It has all the elements required for a good dish: there's mystery in it; it has body—both to look at and to touch, in the mouth; and the flavors are light, rich, balanced, true. It's an original, though it has parents. One parent is at the Gavroche: huîtres Francine, an oyster shell filled with mousse. I replaced the mousse with pasta and the chives with caviar. The other parent is at the Manoir: tagliatelle of langoustines, which is simply pasta topped with langoustine tails. The marriage of those two dishes produced mine. In thirty years' time that dish will still be the same. I'm lucky to have found such a dish in my early twenties; some chefs spend a lifetime searching for a dish like that. Its elegance and excellence make me think of my mother, so I've given it to her. It's the first dish I can really call my own, and I give it to her.

If I had to find two words to describe my food I think I would choose "sensuous" and "feminine." For me they're interlinked, they're very important. I'm a woman's man. I like women because they aren't competitive, because their sensuality is untroubled. They inspire me. Think of the tagliatelle—you'd say a woman had dressed it, and I'm proud of that. That's why I like to taste with my fingers and my hands, because I need a natural, physical relationship with my food, I need the involvement and the understanding that the sense of touch brings. No fingers, no food. When I'm making the mashed potato in the morning, I give myself a fistful. Not a finger, a fistful.

If people would only spend more time tasting what they are cooking instead of worrying about germs, then the quality of their cooking would soar. Licking the

"No one is cooking like it in Britain and I'm here and part of it. I know that to be a great chef I've got to push myself to the very limit every day and every night. That's the only way to do it. I've had to learn to take a lot of flak— but it's made me stronger and built my character. And when boys don't last the pace that makes me feel good because I have and I will."

Stephen Terry,
chef de partie at Harvey's

cake bowl is a precious ritual of childhood that everyone is familiar with, and if people had seen little Marco on television beside his mother licking the cake bowl they would have said "how sweet." Instead they saw big Marco tasting with his fingers and they said "how disgusting." People who can't cope with that lack a passion for life or for food.

Anyone who says they have invented a dish is just bullshitting. You'd need to invent new ingredients before you could invent new dishes. "Good cooking is lots of little things done well," said Fernand Point, and he's absolutely right. The classical marriages are the foundation of all good cooking, which is why I now garnish my pig's foot with mashed potato. The foot is just a sophisticated sausage, after all. Sausage and mash, fish and chips, tomato and basil,

peaches and ice cream, mushrooms and Madeira, they're all classic marriages and no good cook will ever neglect them. But you must use your brain to rethink them, make them relevant, give them a contemporary beauty. Take the lemon tart on my menu. That's a classic lemon tart I first saw made at the Gavroche. All I've done is give it a little extra thought by caramelizing the confectioners' sugar top to make a crunchy layer. It's the most majestic of desserts and it's the only dessert from the classical French repertoire that stands on its own without any frills or garnishes. In fifty years' time it will still be served in the best restaurants.

Another principle of my cooking—and of my life, which is the same thing—is speed and rhythm. Peaks and troughs. We peak, beauty peaks, everything peaks and then it declines, begins to fall apart or rot and decompose. In many kitchens I've worked in, stockpots have bubbled on and on and the stocks have been ruined. I've knocked about an hour off the cooking time for veal stock and about half an hour off the time for chicken stock to stop the flavors getting lost through overcooking. I reduce sauces very rapidly because that's the only way to keep the flavors fresh. I only put a few drops of cream or lemon juice into a sauce at a time because it's important to taste and test each step of the way. You have to follow the development of a taste up the hill until it gets to the peak. Chuck too much in and you could send it over the other side without even being aware of the peak you've missed.

Since I'm talking about principles, here's another: be generous, be extravagant. Without generosity there's no love, and without love there's no understanding. A mean cook is a failed cook. I know I have to watch some

ingredients like foie gras and truffles when I'm cooking but I'd soon go crazy if I had to count the cost all the time. Catering colleges teach students how to be economical, but that's like teaching a singer not to waste her breath by going for the high notes. I think they should give a few lessons in generosity instead.

You know what the one ingredient I don't have in my kitchen is? Time. I wonder what I could achieve if I had it . . . My menu hasn't been built around my talents alone but those of my staff and the time we have. The kitchen is small and we work incredibly hard. Our youth and energy let us compete with places like Tante Claire, the Manoir, Nico's, and the Gavroche. We work our balls off day and night to get the results we do. If I had all the time I wanted, and a kitchen team large enough, I wonder . . . No, it probably wouldn't work. A more relaxed Marco would drop his guard and everything would smash to bits around me.

"Me? My character is still forming, and at this moment I'm in the middle of a revolution with myself. I still haven't truly found myself as a cook and this shows in my food. I'm beginning to blossom; the tagliatelle is the first perfect flower. There will be others."

Marco, 1990

the
heat
of
the

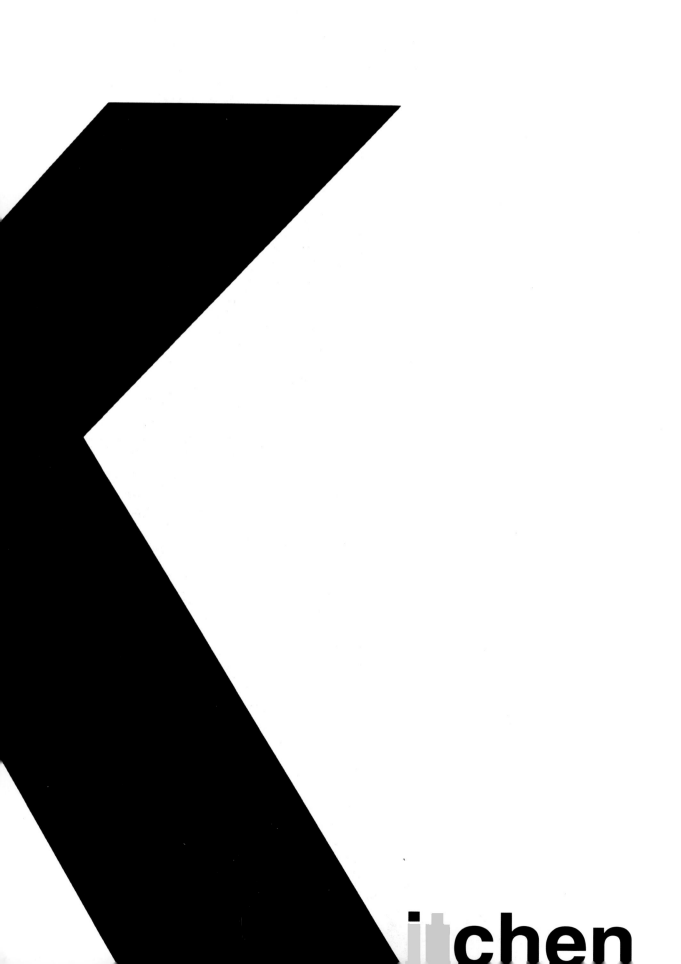

itchen

"I have done nothing apart

from cook for the last ten years. I've

had no social life to speak of,

no real time to myself and

there's been a lot of pain and

suffering getting here. One day I'll

go to France; that'll be my finishing school.

Now it's time to make money, because no money, no love, no food."

"I would say my style is not artistic, but graphic.

"I would say my style is not artistic, but graphic.

It's honest, it's classical, it's natural, it's simple."

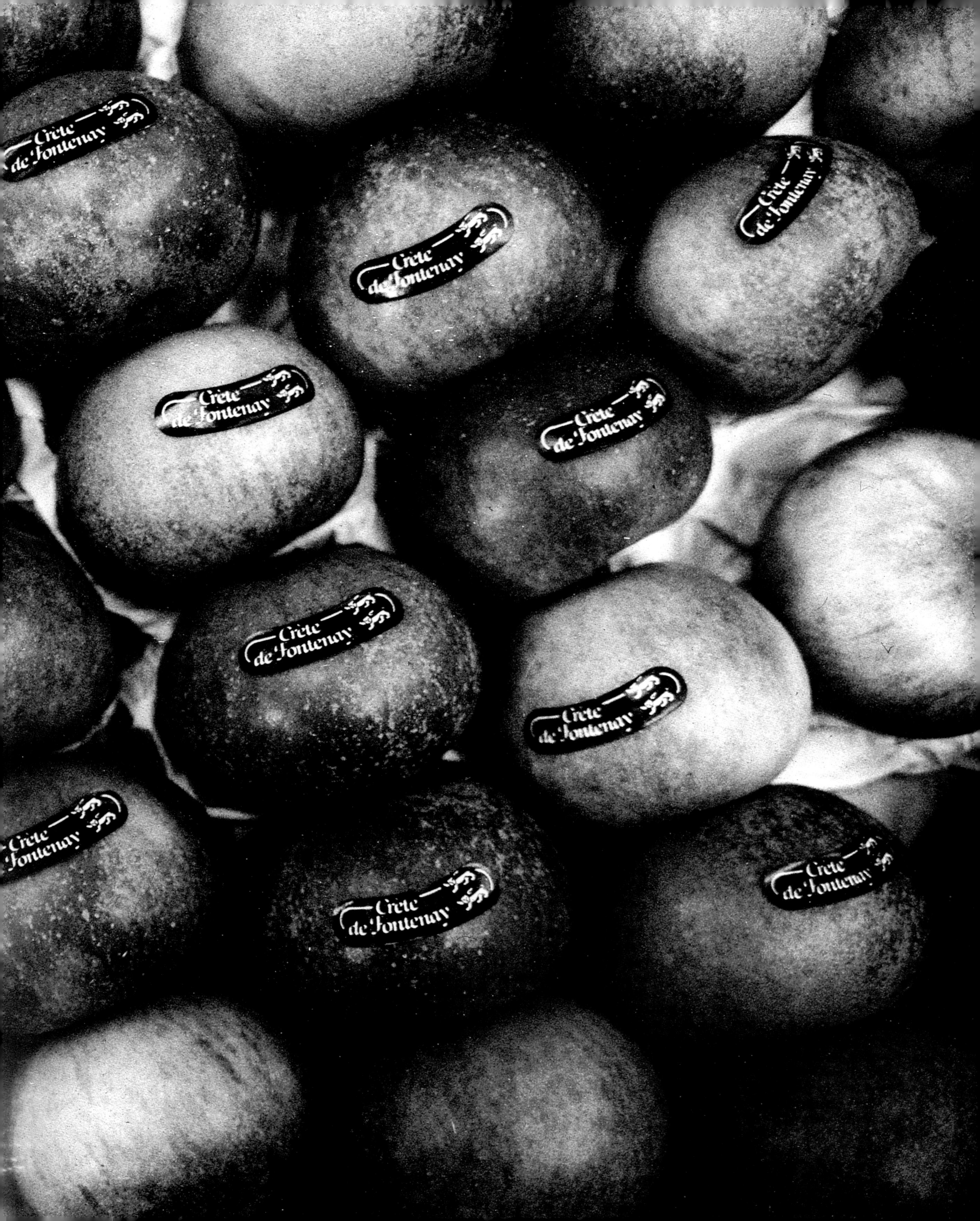
Crete de Fontenay

"I've worked for over ten years for recognition, and now I've got it. I've got money now, but I'm no happier. It's not material things that bring me happiness. Perhaps that's why I work with food, with growing things. I can't make a carrot, and nor can you. It's natural. Without food there's no life. My respect and admiration for life has come from food, through food."

"There are a lot of jobs in life,

but I wonder how many give you the

chance to express yourself like I can here?

I serve what I like, say what I like,

accept the bookings I like, hire and fire the

staff I like. My kitchen is freedom."

"You can tell the scallops are fresh by checking they're closed.

We only deal with hand-dived scallops, not dredged scallops—they

get smashed, damaged. Dredged scallops should be banned."

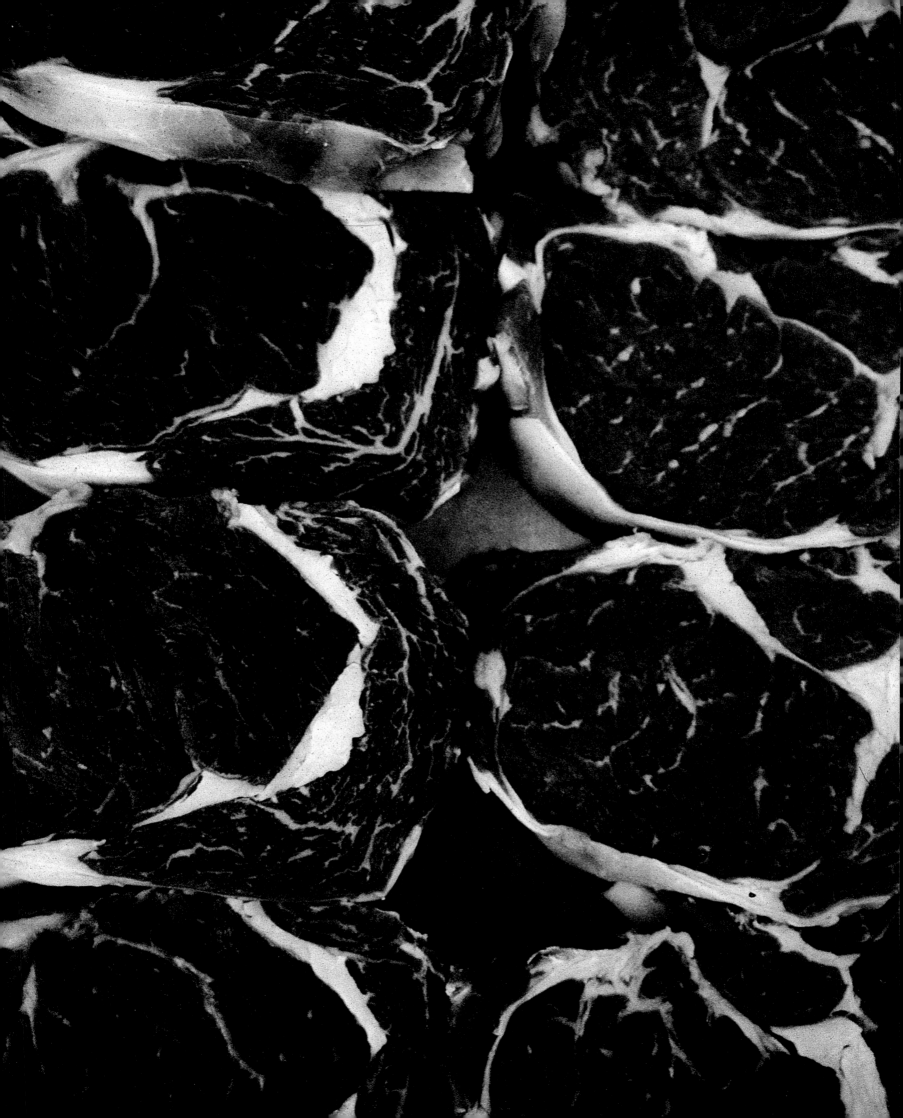

"If I came to your house for dinner an hour late, then criticized all your furniture and your wife's haircut and said all your opinions were stupid, how would you feel? People still come here and expect a three-course meal in an hour. What do they think I do—pull rabbits out of a fucking hat? I'm not a magician."

"Nine out of ten English chefs have their names on their chests.

Just ask yourself how many chefs in this country have

We all wear blue aprons in my kitchen because we're all commis,

Who do they think they are? They're dreamers. They're jokes.

Michelin stars and how many have their names on their jackets.

we're all still learning."

"I was brought up on fruit
in Italy we used to eat
masses of it when you eat
fruit off the tree it tastes ten times better than
normal for the simple reason
that it's warmed by the sun.
The sun is gently cooking
the fruit and bringing out its
natural sweetness."

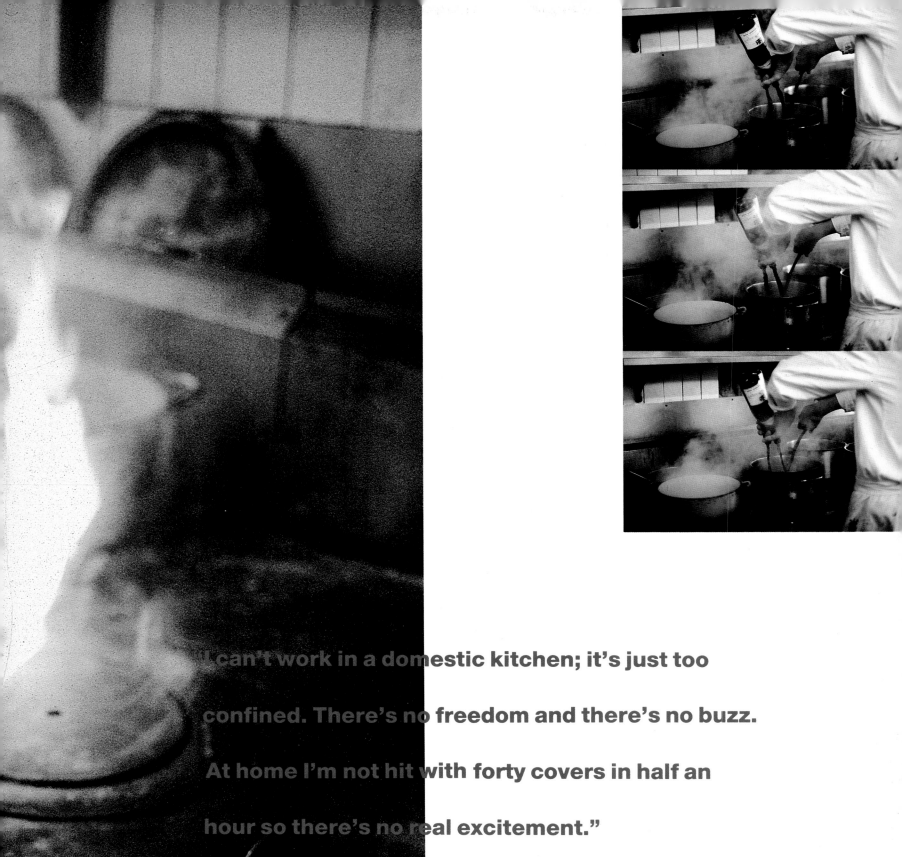

"I can't work in a domestic kitchen; it's just too confined. There's no freedom and there's no buzz. At home I'm not hit with forty covers in half an hour so there's no real excitement."

"When I go out to eat, I'm the ideal customer. I eat the meal and go home and don't complain.

I'd never make a fuss.

But the difference

between me and the

other customers is

that my expectations

are realistic."

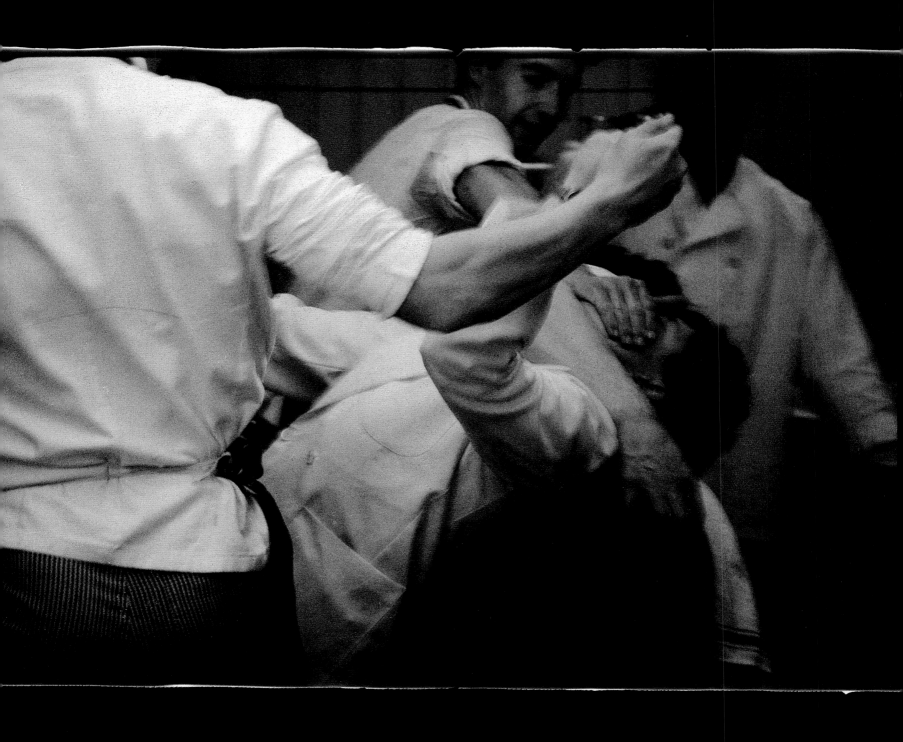

"I'm a man of extremes.

I can't stand things that are diluted — only drinks benefit from that.

I want a hundred per cent of everything, or everybody, or nothing at all."

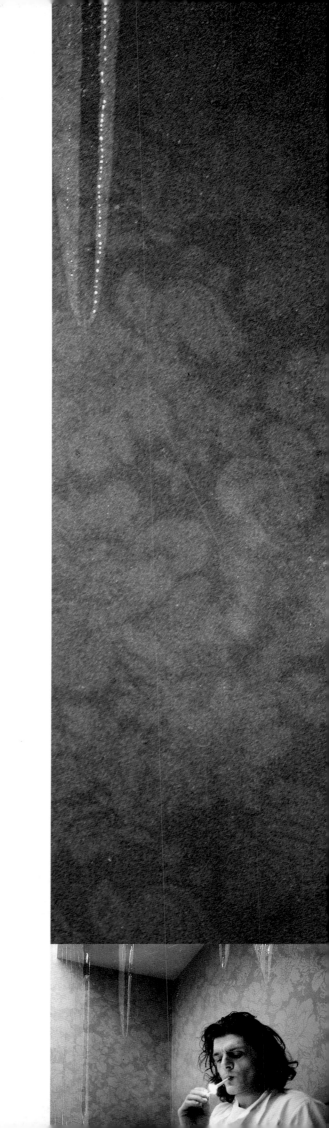

"A lot of people say I look like a rock star or a designer punk.

But I swear it's the job that has carved my face. It's the hours, the stress,

and the pressure. It's not me trying to look like this."

"At the end of the day, it's just food, isn't it? Just food."

the
food
of
the

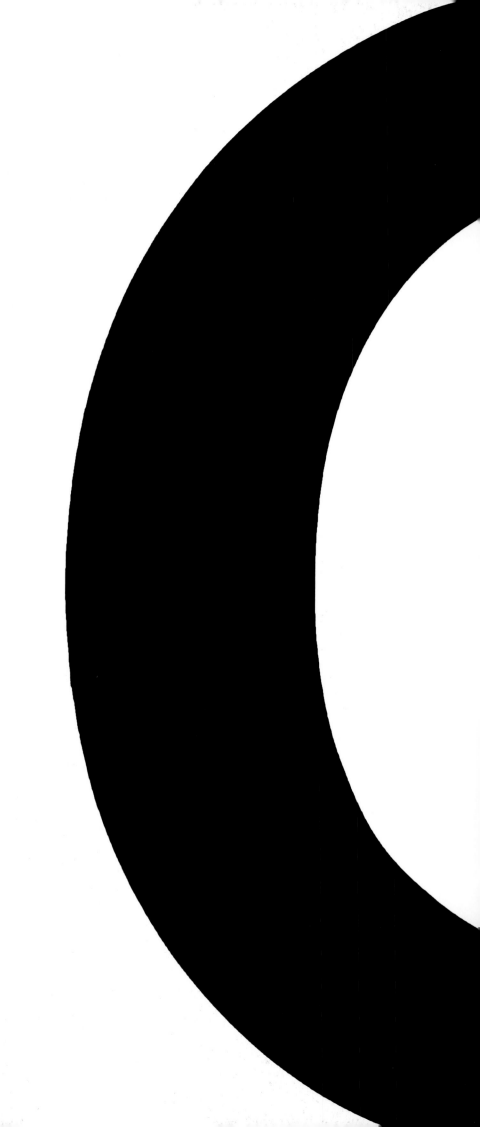

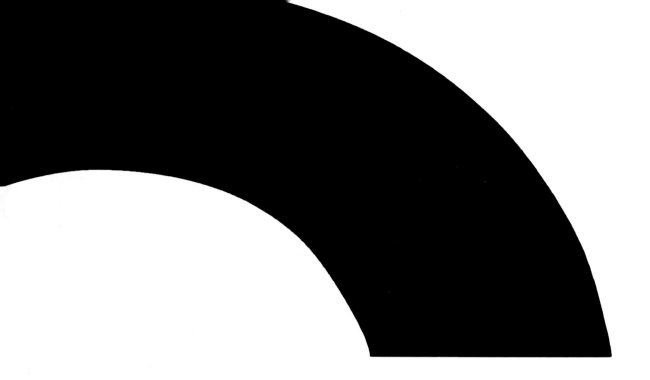

Gods

"I find the lobster a beautiful creature. A lobster is more beautiful to me than most women are. It has this prehistoric gracefulness . . . but it's a machine for killing. Very mechanical, very quick."

one 2–4 lb. lobster, live
1 quantity brunoise of ginger
  (see page 123)
few sprigs of cilantro,
  finely chopped
pinch of cayenne pepper
lemon juice to taste
4 oz. fresh salmon (steak, fillet
  or scrap, skinned and all
  bones removed)
1 egg
salt
4 oz. basic pasta dough
  (see page 119)
1 tbsp. olive oil

for the sauce:
4 tbsp. vegetable stock
  (see page 117)
small piece of butter
2 tsp. sherry vinegar
1 tsp. soy sauce

to serve:
10 fresh shelled scallops, trimmed
  of any coral
1 tbsp. good olive oil
crispy fried leeks
  (see page 120)

TO MAKE THE SAUCE:
1 Bring the vegetable stock to a boil and stir in the butter. Continue to boil until the sauce is reduced to a syrupy consistency.
2 Meanwhile, in a separate small saucepan, combine the sherry vinegar and soy sauce. Bring to a boil and reduce down by about half.
3 Add some of this soy vinegar to the sauce—just a little at a time, as it has such a strong flavor —tasting at each addition, until it is to your liking. It should give the sauce a good caramel color. Keep warm. Reserve a little of the soy vinegar for the cooking of the scallops.

TO MAKE THE LOBSTER RAVIOLI:
1 Bring a large pan of salted water to a boil.
2 Kill the lobster quickly and humanely by sharply inserting a long knife into the cross mark just behind its head. Then twist off the tail and the two claws. Make sure that the pincers have been bound, as they will continue to remain active even after the lobster is dead.
3 Blanch the lobster tail for just 10 seconds and the claws for just 15 seconds in the boiling water to release the membranes from the shells—not to cook the flesh.
4 Remove the lobster flesh from the shells, drain, and pat dry on a clean cloth. Chill in the refrigerator for 1 hour.
5 Chop the chilled lobster into ½ inch cubes. Add the brunoise of ginger, the cilantro, a pinch of cayenne pepper, and some lemon juice. Taste and adjust this seasoning.
6 Put the salmon and the egg in a blender or food processor and blend together to a puree. Season with salt. Add the seasoned lobster, mix thoroughly, and chill until required.
7 Make the ravioli as described on page 120, using the lobster filling.
8 Bring a large pan of water to a rolling boil and add the olive oil. Add the lobster ravioli and poach for 3½ minutes. Drain well and keep warm.

TO MAKE THE GARNISH:
1 Cut each of the scallops across into 2 disks.
2 Dry-fry these in a hot nonstick skillet over a high heat for about 20 seconds on each side. Dribble a few drops of olive oil and a drop or two of the remaining soy vinegar on each scallop during the course of cooking. Be careful not to overcook these delicate items. Cover and keep warm.

TO SERVE:
1 Place the ravioli just above the center of each warmed plate.
2 Place 5 disks of scallop overlapping each other along the bottom of the plate.
3 Decorate the ravioli and scallop with some crispy fried leek.
4 Spoon a little of the sauce on the ravioli and the scallops.

SERVES 4

RAVIOLI OF LOBSTER WITH A BEURRE SOY SAUCE

"Don't make the raviolis too small,

or you'll overcook the lobster flesh in order to get the pasta

correctly cooked, and then you'll lose the lobster's succulence.

The raviolis should be a substantial size."

20 fresh oysters (shelled, retaining their juices and the rounded shell)

for the sauce beurre blanc:
4 shallots, very finely chopped
5 tbsp. white wine vinegar
1 cup unsalted butter, cut into cubes
salt and freshly ground white pepper
lemon juice to taste

to serve:
8 oz. cucumber (as dark a green as you can find)
2 tbsp. butter
8 oz. tagliatelle (see page 119)
fresh seaweed and/or rock salt
2 tbsp. black caviar

TO MAKE THE SAUCE:
1 Put the shallots in a pan with the vinegar and bring to a boil. Continue to boil for a minute or two to drive off the acidity and concentrate the flavors. Add a few drops of cold water and bring the mixture back to a boil.
2 Remove the pan from the heat and gently but quickly beat in the butter piece by piece.
3 Allow the sauce to infuse for 20 minutes. Then season with salt and pepper and a little lemon juice. Pass through a cheesecloth-lined sieve. Taste and adjust seasoning again, if necessary. Warm through just before serving.

TO PREPARE THE TAGLIATELLE AND CUCUMBER GARNISH:
1 Peel and seed the cucumber and cut it into julienne strips about 1½ inches long. Place in a pan with just enough water to cover and half the butter. Bring to just beneath a boil and simmer until the cucumber is just tender. Drain, pat dry, and keep warm.
2 Just before serving, gently warm through the tagliatelle in just enough water to cover, along with the remaining butter and seasoning to taste.

TO COOK THE OYSTERS:
1 Thoroughly scrub clean the rounded oyster shells. Place them in a small pan, cover with water, and bring to a boil. This will both sterilize and warm the shells.
2 Strain the oyster juices to remove any traces of shell. Place the juices in a small pan and bring to a boil with a little water, if needed to cover the oysters. Add the oysters and poach them gently over a low heat until they are just firm to the touch—about 1 minute *only*! Drain the oysters, pat dry with a clean cloth, and keep warm.

TO SERVE:
1 Dress each plate with a bed of either seaweed or rock salt— if you have neither, a little basic mashed potato (see page 121) under each shell will serve to keep the oysters stable. Place the 5 warmed oyster shells securely on each plate.
2 Wind the well-drained tagliatelle around a fork to make a nest to settle inside each shell. Place an oyster on top, then cover with a few strips of cucumber.
3 Spoon the sauce beurre blanc gently over the oysters and then place a few grains of caviar on top of each. Garnish the plate with seaweed if you desire.

SERVES 4

"You've got all the components here of a great dish: simplicity, elegance, graphic impact, texture, fine flavors. It's grand but understated. The dish succeeds in every way. It's not enough for a dish just to have a great flavor; it's only when the taste of a dish equals its visual appeal that you

TAGLIATELLE OF OYSTERS WITH CAVIAR

know you're onto a success. This is one of the few dishes I know which actually does that. It's very rare."

court-bouillon (see page 117)
  or water
80 langoustine tails
4 tsp. salt
4 tsp. sugar
4½–5 lb. baby leeks, trimmed
  weight, cleaned
freshly ground white pepper

for the water vinaigrette:
1¾ cups olive oil
3 tbsp. white wine vinegar
1 cup water
clove of garlic, cut across in half
2 or 3 sprigs of tarragon

to serve:
4 oz. green beans, cleaned
  and trimmed
1 tsp. caviar (optional)

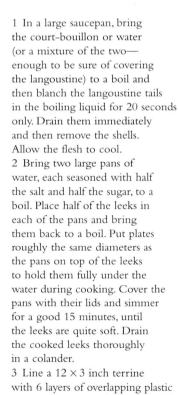

TERRINE OF LEEKS AND LANGOUSTINES, WATER VINAIGRETTE

1 In a large saucepan, bring the court-bouillon or water (or a mixture of the two—enough to be sure of covering the langoustine) to a boil and then blanch the langoustine tails in the boiling liquid for 20 seconds only. Drain them immediately and then remove the shells. Allow the flesh to cool.

2 Bring two large pans of water, each seasoned with half the salt and half the sugar, to a boil. Place half of the leeks in each of the pans and bring them back to a boil. Put plates roughly the same diameters as the pans on top of the leeks to hold them fully under the water during cooking. Cover the pans with their lids and simmer for a good 15 minutes, until the leeks are quite soft. Drain the cooked leeks thoroughly in a colander.

3 Line a 12 × 3 inch terrine with 6 layers of overlapping plastic wrap. (These are necessary to hold the terrine together when it is being weighted later.) Allow a generous overhang all around the edge (sufficient to bring up around the entire dish later).

4 Place a first layer of leeks on the bottom of the lined terrine, alternating white and green ends alongside one another, parallel to the long sides of the terrine. There should be about 10 leeks per layer. Press down firmly and season with pepper. Place the langoustine tails in two rows down the center of the terrine. Pack the gaps and the edges with more leeks and season. Keep alternating layers of leek alone, and langoustine tails with leek filler, seasoning as you go, and finishing with a layer of leeks. This last layer will stand about 1 inch above the edge of the terrine. All the leeks will fit as long as you keep pressing, but this will take a considerable amount of effort and patience and a lot of liquid will ooze out in the process.

5 Fold the overhangs of plastic wrap over, starting with the long sides. Using the point of a sharp knife, prick the plastic wrap around the edge of the terrine at 1 inch intervals (making sure it goes through all the layers!) to let the liquid out during the pressing process.

6 Put the terrine on a baking sheet and place an empty terrine of the same size on top of the covered leeks. Place a second baking sheet on top of the empty terrine and place some 12 lb. weights on top of that (use a lot of canned items if weights are not available). Leave the terrine for 3 hours. During that time, however, unwrap the terrine and press the leeks again by hand a couple of times. Re-wrap and weight again each time, of course, as before. Ideally the pressing process should be overnight, but the terrine should be kept well chilled during that time. (Stand the terrine in a bowl of ice and water if the whole thing won't go in the refrigerator.)

TO MAKE THE WATER VINAIGRETTE:

1 Pour the oil, vinegar, and water into a large bowl. Add the garlic, tarragon, and salt and pepper to taste.

2 Stir the mixture very gently: any brisk movement will cause the vinaigrette to emulsify and the beauty of this dressing is its marbled effect on the plate—separate pearls of oil and water. Cover and strain before use.

TO SERVE:

1 Cut the green beans in half lengthwise, then cut these in half again in the same way. Blanch them for 1 minute in boiling water. Refresh in cold water, drain, and pat dry.

2 Unwrap the terrine and cut it across into 12 slices. Place a slice in the middle of each plate.

3 Arrange the green bean slices in overlapping loops around that.

4 Carefully spoon the vinaigrette over and around the terrine.

5 A few grains of caviar on top of the terrine sets off the green of the leeks and the pink of the langoustine.

SERVES 12

"The guy who should get the credit for this dish is Michele Trama.

He made a terrine of leeks; a wonderful, intelligent concept. I just

took it a little further down the road by adding langoustines."

"You've got the sea in a soup bowl here. I love this dish. When I think about it, it seems natural, full of juices and stocks and fresh scents; when I look at it, it looks posh; when I taste it, it's rich and decadent, incredibly decadent."

8 fresh shelled scallops
12 langoustine tails
3 tbsp. vegetable stock
4 tbsp. julienne of leek
1/2 cup fish velouté
  (see page 118)
1/2 cup jus de nage
  (see page 117)
8 oysters, shelled but juices retained
4 tsp. chopped fresh chervil
salt and freshly ground white pepper
lemon juice to taste

to serve:
36 thin slices of truffle
chopped fresh chervil

1 Cut each scallop into 6 very thin slices.
2 Blanch the langoustine tails in a large pan of rapidly boiling water for 10 seconds only. Drain, leave to cool slightly, and then shell them.
3 In a small pan, bring the vegetable stock to a boil and poach the leek in it until tender but firm. Drain and keep warm.
4 Put the fish velouté, jus de nage, and oyster juices in a pan with the chopped chervil and warm through for 15 seconds, then add the scallops, langoustine tails, and oysters and poach them for about 1 minute. Make sure the liquid does not quite boil during that time. Check the taste and season with salt, pepper, and lemon juice.

TO SERVE:
1 Pour the potage into 4 warmed bowls and sprinkle the leeks over the top.
2 Garnish the tops with the truffle slices and the finely chopped chervil.

SERVES 4

POTAGE OF SHELLFISH WITH TRUFFLE AND LEEK

"Buy the best for

this dish, because the

langoustines and scallops

serve themselves.

You're not doing anything

to them—it's just an assembly job. The art

is their art, it's in the ingredients.

Cucumber and ginger, for example:

beautiful, simple flavors with an

extraordinary affinity for each other.

The whole dish is like that."

1 large cucumber, peeled
24 large langoustine tails
4 oz. basic pasta dough
 (see page 119)
1 egg yolk
8 fresh shelled scallops
1/2 cup jus de nage
 (see page 117)
1/2 cup fish velouté
 (see page 118)
1 oz. fresh ginger root, peeled
 and cut into fine julienne strips
piece of butter
lemon juice to taste
1 star anise
salt and freshly ground white pepper

to serve:
16 tiny sprigs of chervil
4 star anise

1 Seed the cucumber and cut it into 40 tiny long thin barrel shapes.
2 Blanch the langoustine tails in a large pan of rapidly boiling water for 10 seconds only. Drain, leave to cool slightly, and then shell them.

TO MAKE THE RAVIOLI:
1 Prepare the dough as described on page 119. Cut out 4 disks, each about 2 inches in diameter.
2 Mix the egg yolk with a pinch of salt and use it to glaze the pasta circles.
3 Season 4 of the shelled langoustine tails with salt and pepper. Place them each in the center of a pasta circle and fold them over to make a crescent shape. Seal by pinching the edges together. Go over them twice to ensure a good seal. Trim the edges to enhance the crescent shape (use a shaped pastry cutter if you have one).
4 Just before serving, cook the ravioli in a large pan of boiling salted water for 2½ minutes. Drain and keep warm.

TO MAKE THE BLANQUETTE:
1 Cut the scallops across into 2, or 3 if they are large, and place them with the remaining langoustine tails in a large pan along with the jus de nage, the fish velouté, and the ginger. Slowly bring the mixture up to a boil and cook very gently for about 40 seconds. Immediately remove the shellfish from the liquid and keep it warm.
2 Add the cucumber and the piece of butter to the poaching liquid, season to taste with a little lemon juice, pepper, and the star anise, and cook gently until the cucumber is tender but still firm.

TO SERVE:
1 Place a langoustine tail in the center of each of 4 warmed plates and place one of the ravioli on top of it.
2 Arrange the scallops and remaining langoustine tails, alternated, around each of the plates.
3 Remove the star anise from the poaching liquid, check the taste and adjust seasoning, if necessary. Pour equal amounts of poaching liquid, ginger, and cucumber over the shellfish.
4 Garnish each dish with 4 sprigs of chervil and put a star anise on top of each ravioli.

SERVES 4

BLANQUETTE OF SCALLOPS
AND LANGOUSTINES WITH CUCUMBER AND GINGER

1 lb. veal sweetbreads, soaked
in cold water for 2 hours
1 egg yolk
pinch of salt
4 large sheets of phyllo (strudel)
pastry, defrosted if frozen
¼ cup butter
⅓ cup pine nuts
½ cup slivered almonds
salt and freshly ground white pepper
olive oil, for frying

**for the salad and mushroom
garnish:**
16 small pieces each of: oak leaf,
frisée, and lamb's lettuce
1 cup cream vinaigrette
(see page 119)
1 small head of Belgian endive
4 oz. wild black mushrooms
(trompettes-des-morts or horns
of plenty)

to serve:
4 slices of truffle (optional)
16 tiny sprigs of chervil

1 Trim the sweetbreads and gently
remove all membranes and sinews.
Cut into 4 equal slices.
2 Beat the egg yolk together with
the salt. Place each phyllo sheet
on a lightly floured surface and
lightly brush the top with the
egg wash. Cut out three 5 inch
circles from each sheet of pastry
(use an appropriately sized plate
as a guide).
3 Heat a generous amount of the
oil in a large skillet over a high
heat. When the oil is very hot, fry
the phyllo circles until crisp, turn,
and do the same on the other side.
Drain the cooked circles on paper
towels and then store on a wire
rack in a warm place.
4 In a small saucepan, heat half the
butter over a moderate heat. When
the butter has stopped foaming, add
the pine nuts and almonds and
sauté them for about 3 minutes.
Set aside and keep warm.

TO MAKE THE SALAD AND
MUSHROOM GARNISH:
1 Toss the salad leaves in a little
of the vinaigrette. Cut the endive
into fine julienne strips, but
keep separate.
2 Put half of the remaining butter
in a pan over a high heat and cook
the mushrooms until they produce
their liquid. Drain that off and then
cook them for just a little longer in
some fresh butter. Set aside and
keep warm.

TO COOK THE SWEETBREADS:
1 Preheat the oven to 475 F.
Heat a generous amount of oil
in a large skillet over a high heat
until it is smoking (this is essential
to get the crispy exterior to the
sweetbreads). Fry the sweetbreads
until they are golden brown and
crunchy on both sides, but still
moist in the middle.
2 Place the sealed sweetbread slices
between butter papers in a baking
dish and cook in the oven for
about 4 minutes.

TO SERVE:
1 Place a phyllo circle in the center
of each plate (egg-washed side
uppermost). Cut each sweetbread
slice into 2 diagonally, season the
pieces to taste, and place one piece
on the phyllo with a sprinkling
of the pine nuts and almond
mixture and a little vinaigrette.

2 Top this with another phyllo
circle (egg-washed side uppermost)
and place the second piece of
sweetbread on top of that.
Sprinkle again with some nuts
and vinaigrette. Top this with a
final phyllo circle (again, egg-
washed side uppermost). If you
wish, decorate the top with a
small slice of truffle to complete
the "Ascot hat" effect.
3 Arrange the salad in 4 mixed
sprays around the plate, topping
each with some of the endive
julienne and then a sprig of
chervil. Sprinkle the mushrooms
between the salads. Try to
make the arrangement look free,
not too much like a designer's
set piece! Finally spoon a few
drops of the vinaigrette around
the plate.

SERVES 4

"If you can afford to use the truffles, do — sweetbreads and truffles are another of those great, classic combinations. I actually prefer truffles chopped large and glazed, like glistening black jewels, but when I first opened Harvey's

FEUILLANTINE OF SWEETBREADS

I couldn't afford to use them like that. I had to chop them finer

and finer to stretch them further."

SALAD OF RED MULLET, SAUCE GAZPACHO

4 red mullet, cut into fillets with their
    skins intact
1 cup all-purpose flour
seasoning
olive oil, for frying

for the gazpacho sauce:
1 lb. 2 oz. cherry tomatoes,
    stalks removed
2 tsp. white wine vinegar
1 tsp. salt
1 tsp. sugar
1/2 tsp. freshly ground white pepper
6 tbsp. olive oil

**for the brunoise of ratatouille
and salad:**
16 leaves each of: lamb's lettuce,
    frisée, oak leaf
4 tbsp. classic vinaigrette
    (see page 118)
4 tsp. each very finely chopped:
    zucchini (unpeeled), fennel, yellow
    bell pepper (stalks and seeds
    removed), eggplant (unpeeled)

TO MAKE THE SAUCE:
1 In a blender or food processor,
blend the tomatoes (complete
with skins) with the vinegar.
Add the salt, sugar, and pepper
and blend again for 30 seconds.
Keeping the machine running,
add the olive oil slowly until it
is all incorporated.
2 Pass the sauce through a
cheesecloth-lined sieve. Taste and
adjust the seasoning, if necessary.

TO COOK THE FISH:
1 From each fish, cut five 1 inch
squares with their skin still
attached. Season the pieces of fish
well and toss each of them lightly
in flour.
2 Heat some olive oil in a large
skillet over a high heat and
fry the pieces of fish for about
30 seconds on each side. Remove
from the oil and drain on paper
towels. Keep warm.

TO MAKE THE BRUNOISE OF
RATATOUILLE AND SALAD:
1 Dress the salad with the
vinaigrette.
2 In a skillet, put some oil
over a high heat. Cook the
brunoise of ratatouille in it for
only 15 seconds (hence the need
to cut the vegetables finely).
Season to taste.

TO SERVE:
1 Warm the plates and then place
5 teaspoon-size puddles of the
sauce on each plate (the plates
and the fish will warm the sauce).
2 Place a piece of fish in the
middle of each puddle of sauce,
skin-side up.
3 Spoon little piles of the brunoise
of ratatouille between the puddles.
4 Place some delicate heaps of
the dressed salad in the center
of each plate.

SERVES 4

**"There's nothing clever about this; we just borrowed
an idea from the Mediterranean. A bowl of salad, a pot of
ratatouille, a few fried fillets of red mullet, some bread—that's
a great lunch. What more could you want?"**

"Me and my dad used to go down to the old Leeds market and walk past rows and rows of fish stalls; you don't see that any more. At the end was a pea and pie stall. We had pork pies and mushy peas with vinegar on—it was a brilliant combination, those peas and vinegar. All I've done here is use lentils in a sherry vinegar sauce—a lentil's a kind of pea, isn't it?—and the sharpness cuts the foie gras just as it did the pork pies."

1 lb. raw foie gras
salt and freshly ground white pepper

for the cep and lentilles garnish:
¾ quantity lentilles du pays
 (see page 121)
4 garlic cloves, split
½ cup butter
2 tsp. finely chopped shallots
8 oz. fresh ceps

for the sherry vinegar sauce:
½ cup Madeira sauce
 (see page 117)
few drops of sherry vinegar
few drops of heavy cream

TO COOK THE FOIE GRAS:
1 Preheat the oven to 450 F.
Cut the foie gras into 4 escalopes
(thin slices). Season them well
and then dry-fry them in a
nonstick pan over a high heat
until just brown and crunchy
on each side.
2 Place the browned foie gras on
butter paper and cook in the oven
for 3–4 minutes until they are firm
to the touch and releasing some fat.

TO MAKE THE CEP AND LENTILLES
GARNISH:
1 Warm the lentilles gently.
2 Rub the bottom of the skillet
with the garlic and then place
the pan over a moderate heat

and add half the butter. Sweat
the shallots in the butter until
they are translucent.
3 Cut the stalks off the ceps, peel
them and then slice them into
rounds. Wash and pat dry the tops
of the ceps and then slice them
in half. Add the cep stalks and
tops to the shallots and cook over
a high heat until the ceps release
their liquid.
4 Drain the mixture in a colander.
Add the remaining butter to a
clean pan and cook the drained cep
and shallot mixture over a high
heat for about 1 more minute.

TO MAKE THE SAUCE:
1 In a small pan, warm through
the Madeira sauce. Add a few drops
of sherry vinegar to taste, one
or two at a time—tasting after
each addition, as it has a very
powerful flavor!
2 Finish the sauce with a few drops
of cream—no more than that.

TO SERVE:
1 Dress the warmed plates with a
bed of the lentilles and then place a
slice of foie gras on top of each bed.
2 Arrange the ceps around the
plate and spoon the sauce around
the dish—but *not* over the foie gras.

SERVES 4

HOT FOIE GRAS, LENTILLES DU PAYS, SHERRY VINEGAR SAUCE

one 3 lb. rabbit, skinned and
    paunched
salt and freshly ground white pepper
8 oz. puff pastry
oil, for frying
flour, for dusting

for the sauce:
½ cup vegetable stock
¾ cup chicken stock
1 tbsp. olive oil
3 tbsp. butter, cut into cubes
lemon juice to taste
2 tbsp. chopped fresh cilantro

for the vegetable garnish:
1 cucumber, peeled
4 large mouli, peeled
4 large carrots, peeled
12 pencil-thin leeks, trimmed
    and cleaned
2 tbsp. olive oil
6 crushed coriander seeds

to serve:
16 tiny sprigs of chervil

TO PREPARE THE VEGETABLE
GARNISH:
1 Slice the peeled cucumber into
24 pieces which are roughly barrel-
shaped; seed them and then turn,
or shape, them into little barrels.
Do the same with the mouli and
the carrots to make 24 turned
barrels of each. Make 24 tiny
"baguettes" of leek from the 12
leeks by cutting them across in half.
2 Blanch the garnish in a large
pan of boiling water as follows:
1½ minutes for the mouli and
carrots; 1 minute for the leeks;
30 seconds for the cucumber.
Drain them all as they are done,
pat them dry, and then toss them
in the olive oil and crushed
coriander seeds. Keep warm.

TO COOK THE MEAT AND PASTRY:
1 Cut the hind legs off the rabbit
and trim the thigh bone free of
flesh at the end. Cut off the saddle
of rabbit (below the rib cage) and
remove the fillet from either side of
the backbone. Trim and clean each
of the bones on the remaining
saddle to make 2 best end shapes of
rabbit. This should produce: 2 legs,
2 fillets, and 2 best ends, for garnish.

2 Preheat the oven to 450 F.
Season the meat with salt and
pepper. In some oil in a large skillet
over a high heat, brown the meat
on all sides. Drain, place on a butter
paper, and cook in the oven as
follows: 8 minutes for the legs;
6–8 minutes for the saddle fillets;
3 minutes for the best ends.
3 Cut the legs and fillets into
generous slices and divide the best
ends into two. Keep warm.
4 Reduce the oven setting to
425 F. On a lightly floured surface,
roll the pastry out to a thickness
of ¼ inch. Then cut it into 4
rectangular shells 4 × 1½ inches.
Place them on a baking sheet that
has been greased and sprinkled
very lightly with water. Bake in the
oven for 15 minutes, until golden
brown. Keep warm.

TO MAKE THE SAUCE:
1 Combine the vegetable
stock and the chicken stock
in a saucepan and bring them
to a boil. Boil rapidly to reduce
them by about one-quarter.
2 Beat in the olive oil and
the butter. Season with lemon
juice and a little salt and pepper,

tasting as you go. Add the chopped
fresh cilantro.

TO SERVE:
1 Cut a "lid" off the top of each
pastry shell. Spoon out a little of
the soft dough from the middle
of the pastry to make a cavity.
2 Place a pastry shell in the middle
of each of 4 large warmed plates.
Arrange equal portions of the
rabbit in each. Top each with its
respective "lid."
3 Arrange the vegetable garnish
around the plate. Slice the best
ends of rabbit into individual
trimmed chops and use these as
garnish. Spoon the sauce around
the dish and garnish with the sprigs
of chervil.

SERVES 4

"We used to have rabbit stew for tea in Leeds. My dad would

just chop up the rabbit and put it in a pan with celery, carrots,

onions, and bouillon cubes and cook it until it was done—great.

FEUILLETÉ OF ROAST RABBIT, SPRING VEGETABLES, JUS OF CILANTRO

I've loved rabbit ever since; it's something comforting to pick

at over a winter's evening. This is a posh rabbit pie."

2 slices of peeled fresh ginger root,
  cut into fine julienne
12 small calamares, prepared but
  ink retained
10 fresh shelled scallops, each cut
  across in half to make 2 disks
salt and freshly ground white pepper
lemon juice to taste
olive oil, for frying

for the sauce:
1½ cups fish velouté
  (see page 118)
¼ inch piece fresh ginger root,
  peeled and cut into 2 slices
  ¹⁄₁₆ inch thick

TO MAKE THE SAUCE:
1 In a small pan heat the fish
velouté along with the slices of
ginger to just below boiling point.
2 Add the ink from the calamares
and season to taste with salt,
pepper, and lemon juice. Warm
through gently, making quite sure
the sauce does not boil after the
ink has been added. Keep warm.

TO COOK THE CALAMARES:
1 Cover the base of a skillet with
some olive oil and put over a high
heat. When the oil is hot, add the
ginger and the calamares. Cook for
1 minute, turn the heads over, and
cook for 30 seconds more.

2 Season with salt, pepper,
and lemon juice to taste. Drain,
reserve the fried ginger for
garnish, and keep both it and
the calamares warm.

TO COOK THE SCALLOPS:
1 Season the scallops with salt,
pepper, and lemon juice to taste.
2 Cover the bottom of the skillet
with olive oil. Pour off any excess.
Place over a high heat until
smoking and then throw in the
scallops. Cook them for 30 seconds
on one side and then turn them
over and cook for an additional
30 seconds. Remove from the
pan and keep warm.

TO SERVE:
1 Remove the slices of ginger
from the sauce and then pour it
equally over 4 warmed plates.
2 Place 2 heads of calamares
on top of one another in the
center of each plate and arrange
5 scallops around.
3 Split the remaining 4 calamares
heads into tentacles and place them
between the scallops on each plate.
4 Top the central pair of calamares
with the reserved fried ginger.

SERVES 4

"Everyone else looks to France for their inspiration, or maybe China or Thailand nowadays, but I look to Italy. The Italians are great cooks. With this sauce nero, you get a wonderful contrast in color between the scallops and the inky sauce, and it makes you think the taste will be black-and-white, two poles of flavor, but in fact it's very subtle in taste, very nuanced and refined."

FRICASSEE OF SEA SCALLOPS AND CALAMARES WITH GINGER, SAUCE NERO

4 x 8 oz. fresh salmon fillets
   (each about 4 x 4 x ⅜ inch,
   cut from the middle of the salmon)
salt and freshly ground white pepper
lemon juice to taste

for the basil sauce:
2 small shallots, finely chopped

2 tbsp. butter
15 basil leaves, cut into thin
   julienne strips
3 tbsp. Noilly Prat
½ cup fish stock
4 tbsp. heavy cream
1 tbsp. butter

TO MAKE THE SAUCE:
1 In a skillet over a moderate
heat, sweat the shallots in the
butter. When they are translucent
add the basil.
2 Deglaze the mixture with
the Noilly Prat and cook until
almost all the liquid has gone. Add
the fish stock and boil to reduce
by about half. Add the cream
and bring gently back up almost
to a boil.
3 Finish the sauce by adding
the butter in small pieces and
incorporating it by making waves
in the sauce. Check the taste and
adjust the seasoning and add a few
drops of lemon juice as necessary.
Keep warm.

TO COOK THE FISH:
1 Season each piece of salmon
with salt and pepper.
2 Dry-fry the salmon in a
nonstick skillet over a high heat
for 1½ minutes on each side.
Season with a little more pepper
and some lemon juice to taste.

TO SERVE:
Place the fish on a warmed plate
and pour the sauce around it.

SERVES 4

"Here's another essay in simplicity, in cooking a piece of fish well, in making a simple sauce with a light touch. I was shown how to do this dish years ago by Marc Beaujeu when we were with Albert Roux. Marc cooks with a lot of technique—and a lot of grace. You can tell how good a cook is by how well he does the simple things."

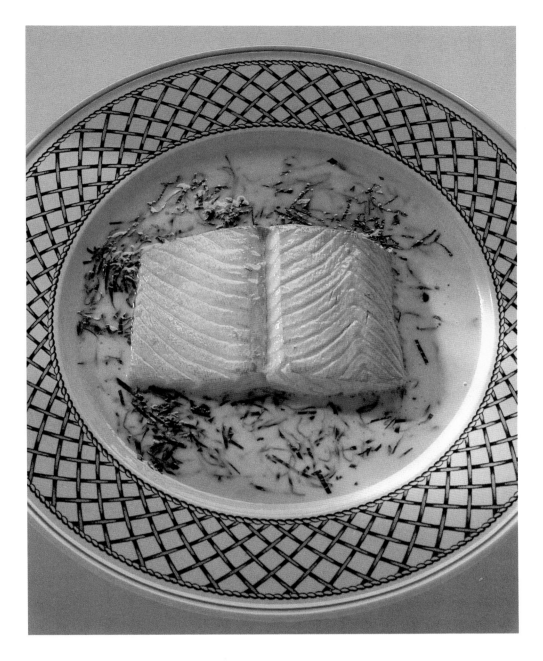

ESCALOPE OF SALMON WITH BASIL

"A sea bass is a beautiful fish. You don't have to do much to it, but you should give it your intelligence. The fashion is for sea bass with ginger, but I think that's wrong for such a Mediterranean fish. Whereas an essence of sweet red pepper is very fine, very subtle, and true to its origins. It's a lovely marriage."

one whole sea bass, weighing
   about 2½ lb.
few drops of olive oil
few drops of lemon juice
4 basil leaves
salt and freshly ground white pepper

**for the mousseline of scallop
   stuffing:**
4 oz. fresh shelled scallops
pinch of salt and cayenne pepper
6 tbsp. heavy cream, chilled
lemon juice, to taste

for the pasta rostis:
4 tbsp. oil
4 oz. tagliatelle
   (see page 119)

for the sauce:
4 red bell peppers, cored, seeded,
   and quartered
3 tbsp. olive oil
4 shallots, finely sliced

2 basil leaves
1 star anise
½ head of garlic, cut across to halve
   each clove
2 tbsp. white wine vinegar
¾ cup Noilly Prat
1¼ cups vegetable stock
⅔ cup water
few drops of olive oil
2 tbsp. butter
1 tbsp. fresh orange juice

for the ratatouille garnish:
1 zucchini
1 eggplant
1 red bell pepper
1 segment of bulb fennel
olive oil, for frying

TO MAKE THE MOUSSELINE OF
SCALLOP STUFFING:
1 Process the scallops in a blender
for 1 minute.

2 Add a pinch of salt and a pinch
of cayenne pepper and work for a
few more seconds.
3 With the blender still running,
start adding the cream very slowly
in a steady trickle. Once all the
cream has been incorporated, turn
the mixture out into a bowl and
add a few drops of lemon juice
to taste.
4 Chill the mousseline for at least
1 hour before use.

TO MAKE THE PASTA ROSTIS:
1 Heat 4 tbsp. of oil in a large
skillet over a moderate heat.
Arrange four 4 inch metal muffin
rings in the pan. When the oil is
very hot, divide the well-drained
pasta between the rings and flatten
the pasta piles into "nests."
2 Cook for a few minutes, until
crispy and golden brown on the
underside. Remove the rings,

turn the rostis over, and cook the
other side in the same way.
3 Drain on a wire rack and reheat
in a hot oven when required.

TO MAKE THE SAUCE:
1 Cut the pepper roughly into
strips. Heat the oil in a large skillet
over a moderate heat and cook
the pepper strips along with the
shallots, basil, star anise, and garlic
for about 5 minutes, until softened
but not browned.
2 Add the vinegar and cook for
a minute or two to drive off the
acidity and bring out the flavor of
the peppers. Add the Noilly Prat
and cook rapidly over a high heat
to reduce to a syrupy consistency.
3 Add the vegetable stock and
water and simmer for 20 minutes.
Remove the star anise and garlic.
4 Put the sauce in a blender
or food processor and blend.

FILLET OF SEA BASS WITH RATATOUILLE AND AN ESSENCE OF RED PEPPERS

Strain through a cheesecloth-lined sieve 3 or 4 times, rinsing the cheesecloth each time. Keep warm.
5 Just before serving, reduce the sieved sauce a little (down to a coating consistency), and add a few drops of olive oil, 1 or 2 pieces of butter, and a little orange juice. Check the taste and adjust the seasoning and add more orange juice, if necessary. Keep warm.

TO COOK THE FISH:
1 Remove all the tough scales from the fish skin using the back of a knife pulled against their "grain."
2 With the point of the knife, make an incision behind the head, just at the back of the fins. Then cut along one side of the backbone to the tail in one steady movement. Using stroking movements of the knife, gradually ease the flesh away

from the bone on that side. Repeat these operations on the other side of the fish, but this time working from tail to head. Cut off any fins and, using tweezers, remove any bones from the fillets. Cut each fillet across in half.
3 Place the fillets skin-side down on a board. Using a very sharp knife, make a lengthwise cut down the middle of the fillet, taking care not to cut any deeper than halfway through the flesh. Then gradually cut away the flesh from the skin either side of this cut to make a double flap or cavity for the stuffing.
4 Spread the mousseline of scallop stuffing evenly over the inner halves of the opened-out fish fillets. Carefully fold back over the flesh of the outer flaps. The mousseline should not be visible once this is done.

5 Lay out 4 large pieces of plastic wrap on a work surface and rub each of them lightly with olive oil, then season with salt and pepper and a little lemon juice. Place the fillets, skin-side down, on the plastic wrap. Top each fillet with a basil leaf and a few more drops of olive oil and salt and pepper to taste. Wrap the fillets very carefully in the plastic wrap, making sure that they are completely sealed and that the shape of the fillet is maintained.
6 Steam the fillet parcels in a single layer in a steamer for 5 minutes. (Putting them on butter papers makes them easier to handle during this process.)

TO MAKE THE RATATOUILLE GARNISH:
1 Peel off the skins of the zucchini, eggplant, and bell pepper.

Cut these skins and the fennel into ¾ inch squares.
2 Just before serving, fry them in a little olive oil over a high heat for a minute or two until they just begin to soften. Drain and season with salt and pepper.

TO SERVE:
1 Unwrap the fish from the plastic wrap, rub a few more drops of olive oil into the skin side, and season it with a little salt.
2 Place a reheated pasta rosti in the center of each of 4 warmed plates. Then place the fillets, skin-side uppermost, on top of the rostis.
3 Spoon the sauce around the plates and then drop the freshly cooked ratatouille garnish into the sauce around the plate, skin-side up.

SERVES 4

"This is a powerful, visual selection of fishes all roasted to order and served with a red wine sauce. The colors, sizes, shapes, and textures are all different, graphic, full of impact—it's an exciting dish."

4 fresh shelled scallops
4 fresh oysters, shelled but reserving
   their juices and curved shells
4 x 1 inch squares of turbot fillet,
   skinned
4 x 1 inch squares of sea bass fillet
   (with skin)
4 x 1 inch squares of salmon fillet,
   skinned
4 x 1 inch squares of red mullet fillet
   (with skin)
olive oil, for frying

for the sauce:
1 cup basic red wine stock
   (see page 116)
1/2 cup vegetable stock
2 tbsp. heavy cream
1 star anise
salt and freshly ground white pepper

for the garnish:
1 cucumber, peeled and seeded
3 large carrots, peeled
12 small potatoes, peeled
2 tbsp. butter
7 cups fresh spinach, washed
   and trimmed
white of 1 leek

TO MAKE THE SAUCE:
1 In a medium saucepan, bring the
2 stocks to a boil and cook rapidly
until they are reduced by one-third.
Taste and adjust the seasoning.
2 Just before serving, add the
heavy cream and star anise and
allow to infuse for 1 minute.
Remove the star anise, taste,
and adjust the seasoning again,
if necessary.

TO PREPARE THE GARNISH:
1 Cut and shape the cucumber,
carrots, and potatoes each into 24
1 inch-long barrels of roughly the
same circumference.
2 In a large pan of boiling water,
blanch these vegetables separately
until each are tender but still
firm. Just before they are needed,
reheat the cucumber, carrots, and
potatoes in just enough emulsion
of water with a piece of butter to
cover them.

3 Pick out the 8 best-looking large
whole spinach leaves, dry-fry them
over a high heat until they are just
soft and keep warm. Melt the
remaining butter in a large skillet
over a high heat and fry the rest of
the spinach for 3 minutes, turning
it frequently. Season with salt and
drain very thoroughly. Make the
cooked spinach into 4 parcels
wrapped in 4 of the reserved leaves.
4 Scrub the curved oyster shells
and place them in boiling water
for a few minutes to sterilize and
warm them through.
5 Strain and gently warm through
the reserved oyster juices.
6 Cut the leek white into fine
julienne and blanch in boiling
water for 1 minute. Drain
thoroughly and pat dry with
paper towels.

TO COOK THE FISH:
1 Put some oil in a large skillet
over a moderate to high heat.
2 When the oil is just beginning
to smoke, fry the scallops, oysters,
turbot, and sea bass for 1 minute.
Then add the salmon and red
mullet and fry for 1 more minute.
Turn all the fish over and fry for
an additional minute.

TO SERVE:
1 Position the pieces of fish and
scallops around 4 warmed plates.
In the spaces between the fish,
arrange the barrels of vegetables.
2 Place the warmed oyster shells
at the top of each plate. In each,
make a bed for the oyster with the
remaining whole spinach leaves.
Place the oysters on the spinach
beds and pour the reserved oyster
juices over them. Garnish the
oysters with the julienne of leek.
3 Place the parcel of spinach in
the middle of the plate.
4 Spoon the sauce over the fish
and the spinach parcels.

SERVES 4

NAVARIN OF FISH

NAGE OF SOLE AND LANGOUSTINE WITH CARROT

"This is a very pretty dish,

orange, pink, and white and perfumed.

You eat it with your eyes and nose first. If a

dish doesn't look good and smell good,

then it will never taste good."

4 large dover sole fillets, skinned
20 langoustine tails
²/₃ cup jus de nage
  (see page 117)
40 cilantro leaves, finely chopped
¹/₃ cup butter
2 oz. carrot, cut into thin julienne
  strips about 1¹/₂ inches long
lemon juice
salt and freshly ground white pepper

1 Cut the sole into "goujonettes" ¹/₂ inch wide and 1 inch long (roughly 6 per fillet to give 24 in all).
2 Blanch the langoustine tails in a large pan of rapidly boiling water for 10 seconds only. Remove them quickly from the water, allow to cool slightly, and then shell them.
3 In a large pan, bring the jus de nage almost to a boil and add the sole goujonettes. Cook them gently for 1¹/₂ minutes, turning them frequently and carefully.
4 Add the cilantro and allow it to infuse for about 5 seconds or so before adding the langoustine tails. Bring the liquid back up to just below boiling point and cook gently for an additional 1¹/₂–2 minutes until opaque, again turning the fish and seafood frequently and carefully to ensure even cooking.
5 Remove the fish and langoustine tails from the liquid and keep them warm.

TO MAKE THE SAUCE:
1 Strain off and discard half the poaching liquid, add the butter, and incorporate it by making waves in the liquid.
2 Add the carrot julienne and lemon juice and seasoning to taste. Leave on a gentle heat for about 1 minute to allow the carrot to soften slightly.

TO SERVE:
1 On each of 4 warmed plates, build the sole goujonettes and the langoustine tails into pyramids.
2 Pour the sauce over the pyramids.

SERVES 4

4 x 1½ lb. live lobsters
7 cups court-bouillon (see page 117)

for the sauce:
1 cup jus d'homard (see page 118)
¾ cup classic vinaigrette
 (see page 118)
1 tbsp. butter
salt and freshly ground white pepper

for the garnish:
48 very thin baby leeks, trimmed
8 oz. tagliatelle (see page 119)
piece of butter

TO MAKE THE SAUCE:
1 Reduce the jus d'homard
by one-third over a high heat,
yielding about ¾ cup.
2 Beat in the vinaigrette and
finish with a little butter,
incorporating it by making
waves in the sauce. Taste and
adjust the seasoning, if necessary.
Keep warm.

TO MAKE THE GARNISH:
1 In a pan of boiling salted water,
cook the leeks until just soft.
Drain thoroughly.
2 Just before serving, reheat
them in an emulsion of butter
and water, seasoned with salt
and pepper.
3 Reheat the tagliatelle in the
same way and then form into
4 balls as described on page 119.

TO COOK THE LOBSTERS:
1 Humanely kill the lobsters as
described on page 56. Separate the
tail and claws and reserve the heads
for garnish, if desired.
2 In a large pan, bring to a boil
the court-bouillon (enough to
cover the lobsters—you can add
some water to the court-bouillon
if necessary). Poach the lobsters
gently in it for 3½ minutes.
Drain and then carefully remove
the flesh from the shells in whole
pieces (1 tail and 2 claw pieces
per lobster).

TO SERVE:
1 Arrange 12 leeks in a bed
on the lower part of each of
4 warmed plates, with the white
bases radiating outward.
2 Cut the lobster tails into
3 lengthwise and fan these
out over the beds of leek.
3 Place the 2 claws at 4 o'clock
and 10 o'clock respectively on
each plate, with the lobster head
between them if using.
4 Place a ball of pasta at the base
of the lobster tail fan or serve it
on a separate side plate.
5 Spoon the sauce over the
lobster flesh.

SERVES 4

"When lobsters are in tanks

they feed on their own flesh.

You can have a majestic

beast fished out for you,

but it may be on its last legs, it may have almost eaten itself up,

inside. You can tell that by feeling the weight of its tail.

If it feels heavy and solid then you know it's a good lobster;

if it's light, then it's been in the tank for a while.

This dish is so simple that you

LOBSTER WITH ITS OWN VINAIGRETTE

need good lobsters. It's just lobster with lobster."

4 x 6 oz. fillets of turbot,
　skinned
salt and freshly ground white pepper
lemon juice to taste

for the sauce:
1/2 cup fish stock
1 tbsp. olive oil
1/4 cup butter
2 tbsp. grained mustard

for the garnish:
2 large celery sticks, trimmed and
　peeled but green leaves retained
whites of 4 medium leeks
1 cup dry white wine
12 very small baby leeks, trimmed
　and cleaned
2 tbsp. butter
4 scallops
lemon juice to taste
4 oz. basic pasta dough
　(see page 119)

TO MAKE THE CHOUCROUTE OF
CELERY AND LEEK:
1　Cut the celery and 2 of the
leek whites into very thin julienne
strips (about 1/16 inch thick and
1 1/2 inches long).
2　Put them into a saucepan with
just enough white wine to cover.
Bring this to a boil, take off the
heat, and allow to infuse.
3　Drain and season to taste
before serving.

TO PREPARE THE LEEKS:
1　Cut the baby leeks into julienne
strips. Poach them in boiling water
for about 1 minute. Drain and
refresh in cold water.
2　Just before serving, warm the
leek through in just enough
seasoned emulsion of butter in
water to cover.

TO PREPARE THE RAVIOLI:
1　Finely chop the 2 remaining
leek whites and then sweat them
in the remaining butter over a low
heat until soft but not browned.
Season, drain, and allow to cool.
2　Puree 1 of the scallops in a
blender or food processor. Chop
the other 3 into very small pieces.
3　When the leeks have cooled,
mix them with the scallop puree
and the chopped scallops. Season
the mixture with salt and pepper
and a drop or two of lemon juice.
4　Make the ravioli as described on
page 120 but instead of cutting
8 large circles of dough, use a
pastry cutter to cut out 40 smaller

circles about 1 1/4 inches in diameter.
Place the filling in small piles on
one side of each of these disks
and then fold each over to make
crescents. Pinch the edges all round
to seal them. Trim, if necessary, and
then pinch round the edges again
to ensure a good seal.
5　Poach the ravioli in boiling
water as described on page 120.

TO MAKE THE SAUCE:
1　Bring the fish stock to a boil and
beat in the olive oil and the butter.
2　Add the tiny amount of
mustard and check the taste.
Season with salt and pepper
and a little lemon juice, tasting
all the time. Keep warm.

TO COOK THE FISH:
1　Season the fillets with salt
and pepper and a few drops of
lemon juice.
2　Steam the fillets in a single layer
in a steamer for 3 1/2–4 minutes.

TO SERVE:
1　Place piles of the baby leek
julienne on each of 4 warmed
plates. Place the turbot fillet on
top of the bed of leeks.
2　Place 10 ravioli side by side
along the top of each plate and
the pile of choucroute on top of
the fish.
3　Spoon the sauce around the
plate and garnish the ravioli with
the reserved celery leaves.

SERVES 4

"This is me tinkering with another classical marriage: turbot and mustard. It was a classic that all the best restaurants did 10 or 15 years ago; it's rare now, but I didn't invent it. You can't reinvent the wheel: all you can do is put new tires on it. The mustard gave me the sauce, and then it set me thinking about sausages, which suggested a choucroute. And then I added the shellfish. The turbot doesn't object: she's

TURBOT WITH BABY LEEKS, A RAVIOLI OF SCALLOPS,
CHOUCROUTE OF CELERY WITH A GRAIN MUSTARD SAUCE

big enough to take it all. She doesn't get easily offended."

4 whole red mullet, each weighing
   about 6 oz.
salt and freshly ground white pepper
flour, for dusting
olive oil, for frying

for the sauce:
½ cup jus de nage
   (see page 117)
4 segments of pink grapefruit
1 tbsp. olive oil
8 cilantro leaves, finely chopped
⅓ cup butter

for the garnish:
8 segments of orange
8 segments of pink grapefruit
8 segments of lemon
zest of 2 lemons, cut into
   julienne strips
2 inch piece fresh ginger root, peeled
   and cut into fine julienne strips
½ cup stock syrup
   (see page 123)
1 tbsp. white wine vinegar
4 sticks of celery, trimmed, peeled,
   and cut into fine julienne strips
piece of butter

TO MAKE THE GARNISH:
1 Put the citrus segments to
warm in a bowl above the stove.
2 In boiling water, blanch the
julienne of lemon and ginger
briefly together. Refresh them
in cold water. Then blanch them
and refresh again. Drain.
3 In a fresh pan cover the julienne
with just enough stock syrup to
cover and bring this to a boil.
Poach the julienne for about
15 minutes. Then add just enough
vinegar to give a balanced sweet-
and-sour taste. Allow to infuse.
4 Cook the julienne of celery in
just enough emulsion of butter
in water to cover, until they are
cooked but not soft.

TO MAKE THE SAUCE:
1 Boil the jus de nage in a small
saucepan. Beat in the grapefruit
segments until they dissolve (only
tiny cells of juice will remain).
2 Beat in the olive oil and the
chopped cilantro. Keep warm.
3 Just before serving, finish by
adding the butter in small pieces,
incorporating it by making waves
in the sauce.

TO COOK THE FISH:
1 Fillet the fish into 8 fillets as
described on page 75, but leaving
the skin intact.

2 Season and flour the fish lightly.
Fry the fillets in hot olive oil in a
large skillet over a high heat for
1 minute on each side.

TO SERVE:
1 Make a bed of celery in the
middle of each warmed plate
and place 2 fillets on each bed,
skin-side upward.
2 Garnish the fish with the
warmed citrus fruit segments—
one of each on each fillet. Sprinkle
a little drained zest of lemon
and ginger along the length
of each fillet.
3 Spoon the sauce around
the dish.

SERVES 4

"This is a nice clean dish for a summer's evening. It's a dish for a lady; clean, not robust. I don't think women should eat robust dishes. Women are much cleaner creatures than men, so they need a cleaner diet."

"I buy 4–6 oz. red mullet to keep a light flavor; the bigger they get, the stronger the flavor,

RED MULLET WITH CITRUS FRUITS

and a really big one tastes very earthy."

"This is my favorite dish. If it had been a painting it would hang in the Tate. It's simple and earthy, but it's also elegant and intelligent. You can't take it any further. It's a complete meal. It's not a recipe for talking about; it's a meal to be eaten."

6 pigs' feet (from the back
   legs only)
1 tbsp. oil
2 carrots, peeled and cubed
1 stick of celery, trimmed and cubed
1 onion, cubed
1 cup dry white wine
3 cups veal stock
   (see page 116)
sprig of thyme
1/2 bay leaf
salt and freshly ground white pepper

for the filling:
1 1/2 oz. dried morels
1 lb. 6 oz. veal sweetbreads
1/2 onion, diced
1 1/4 cups chicken mousse
   (see page 120)
olive oil, for frying

for the sauce:
2 chicken legs
4 oz. mushrooms, sliced
4 oz. shallots, chopped
1/2 head of garlic, sliced across to
   halve each clove
sprig of thyme
1/2 bay leaf
1 1/2 tbsp. sherry vinegar
1 1/2 tbsp. cognac
1 3/4 cups Madeira
2 1/2 cups veal stock (see page 116)
3/4 cup chicken stock
2/3 cup water
4 dried morels
lemon juice to taste
few drops of cream
piece of butter
olive oil, for frying

for the garnish:
72 wild mushrooms, chopped
2 tbsp. butter
72 roasted button onions
   (optional, see page 121)
basic mashed potato (see page 121)

1 Soak the pigs' feet in cold water for 24 hours. Drain and pat dry. Singe off any remaining hairs, particularly between the toes. Scrape off the singed stubble and any stray hairs with a knife.
2 Slit the underside of each foot lengthwise, starting at the ankle end. Cut the main tendon and then start to work off the skin by cutting around it with a sharp knife close to the bone. (Remember that the foot skin is effectively going to form a sausage skin, so be careful not to tear it!)
3 Pull the skin right down and cut through the knuckle joint at the first set of toes. Continue to pull the skin off to the last toe joint. Snap and twist off the bones and discard them.
4 Preheat the oven to 425 F. In the oil in a heavy casserole dish, fry the carrot, celery, and onion over a moderate heat for about 2 minutes. Add the skins, skin-side down, and the wine and boil until the wine is reduced by about half.
5 Add the stock, thyme, and bay leaf. Bring to a boil, cover,

and cook in the oven for about 3 hours. During that time, shake the casserole from time to time to prevent the skins from sticking to the pan. Remove the skins from the cooking liquid and allow to cool. They should be a wonderful oak brown color.

TO MAKE THE FILLING:
1 Soak the morels in cold water for 10 minutes. Drain and rinse. Repeat this process once more.
2 Remove the sinew and membranes from the sweetbreads, saving the trimmings for the sauce. Cut the sweetbreads into cubes and fry these in very hot oil in a large skillet over a high heat until they are golden brown with a crunchy texture.
3 Add the soaked morels and the onion and cook for 1 minute only. (Remember this mixture is to be cooked again in the trotter.) Season well with salt and white pepper, drain the mixture through a colander and allow to cool.
4 When the mixture is cool, stir in just enough chicken mousse to bind the mixture

together. Taste and adjust the seasoning again, if necessary.

TO MAKE THE SAUCE:
1 In some oil in a large skillet over a moderate heat, fry the chicken legs and sweetbread trimmings until they are golden brown but not cooked through.
2 Add the mushrooms, shallots, garlic, thyme, and bay leaf and stir well. Deglaze the contents of the pan with the sherry vinegar, cooking to drive off the acidity. Deglaze in the same way with the cognac.
3 Add the Madeira and reduce the mixture until it has a caramelized appearance. Add the stocks and water to cover the bones and vegetables. Drop in the dried morels and simmer the mixture for 20 minutes. Pass the sauce through a sieve or cheesecloth several times, reserving the morels for garnish if you desire. Keep warm.
4 Just before serving, reduce the sieved stock just a little to a coating consistency. Taste and adjust the seasoning. Add a few drops of

BRAISED PIG'S FOOT "PIERRE KOFFMANN"

lemon juice and one or two drops of cream. Then add a piece of butter and a little pepper. Taste the sauce as you go while adding all these, to get exactly the right taste for you!

TO STUFF THE PIGS' FEET:
1 Cut 6 large squares of kitchen foil big enough to wrap and seal the stuffed pigs' feet.
2 Butter one side of each of the pieces of foil before placing the foot whole skin side down. Pick out the little pieces of fat inside the skin.
3 Divide the stuffing mixture between the 6 pigs' feet. There should be sufficient stuffing to give each of the feet enough

bulk to hold its original shape.
4 Roll the foil tightly around the foot, making a sausage shape, and twist at either end to seal them securely. Put the parcels in the refrigerator for about 15 minutes to set the foot.
5 In a large pan of boiling water, poach the pigs' feet for about 12 minutes.

TO MAKE THE GARNISH:
1 Cook the wild mushrooms in half the butter in a large skillet over a high heat until they produce their liquid.
2 Drain the mushrooms and then cook them again for a minute or two in the remaining butter. Keep warm.

TO SERVE:
1 Remove the pigs' feet parcels from the poaching water and unwrap them.
2 Carefully place the pigs' feet, intact skin side up, on the 6 warmed plates.
3 If using, place 12 onions on each plate, in lines above and below the pig's foot. Sprinkle the mushrooms over the foot.
4 Place a pool of mashed potato alongside the pig's foot and dot it with slices of the morels reserved from the sauce.
5 Coat the pigs' feet with the sauce and spoon more sauce around the plate.

SERVES 6

4 plump pigeons, dressed but
 giblets retained
4 juniper berries
4 sprigs of thyme
salt and freshly ground white pepper
oil, for frying

for the sauce:
1 chicken carcass
3 tbsp. oil
8 shallots, finely chopped
4 oz. button mushrooms, sliced
1/2 head of garlic, cut across to halve
 each clove
sprig of thyme
1/2 bay leaf
1 tbsp. sherry vinegar
1 1/2 tbsp. cognac
1 3/4 cups Madeira
6 tbsp. dry white wine
3/4 cup veal stock (see page 116)
3/4 cup chicken stock
1 1/4 cups water
few chopped truffles
lemon juice to taste (optional)
piece of butter (optional)

for the garnish:
1 lb. button mushrooms
 (or mixed types of mushrooms)
1/3 cup butter
4 oz. shallots
1/2 garlic clove
sprig of thyme
2 tbsp. chicken mousse
 (see page 120)
4 oz. basic pasta dough
 (see page 119)
8 baby turnips with their stalks
2 tbsp. water
lentilles du pays (see page 121)
4 potato rostis (see page 121)
confit of garlic (see page 122)
4 thin slices of truffle
roasted button onions
 (see page 121)

1 Chop off the wing tips of the pigeons and save these, with the livers, hearts, and necks, for the sauce. Singe away any remaining feathers. Place a juniper berry, a sprig of thyme, and a little salt in each cleaned cavity and keep the birds in the refrigerator until they are required.
2 Preheat the oven to 450 F. Fry the pigeons in oil in a large pan to brown them on all sides and then roast in the oven for about 8 minutes. Allow them to rest upturned on their breasts for 5 minutes after they come out of the oven so that all their juices will run into the breast flesh. Cut off

the legs and then the breasts and keep them warm between butter papers in the switched-off oven.

TO MAKE THE RAVIOLI:
1 Cut the mushrooms into quarters and sauté them in a little butter with the shallots, garlic, and thyme. After about 3 minutes drain this mixture through a colander and then cook it again in some fresh butter in the same pan. Continue to sauté until the shallots are soft.
2 Strain again and then place the mixture in the center of a clean dish towel and then use the towel to squeeze the mixture tightly to remove all the moisture. Chop the dry mixture finely and allow to cool. When cool, blend all but 4 large spoonfuls of it with the chicken mousse. Reserve the remaining mixture for garnish and keep warm.
3 Using the mixture blended with the mousse as a filling, prepare the ravioli as described on page 120. Blanch them for a minute or two to set them. Then, just before serving, plunge them once again in boiling salted water for 2 minutes.

TO PREPARE THE BABY NAVETS:
1 Trim the turnips until they are roughly equal in size (about 1 inch across). Place with their stalks uppermost in a pan and cover

with boiling water. Cook over a high heat for 5 minutes. Drain and refresh in cold water.
2 When cool, peel off their fine skins.
3 Just before serving, melt 2 tbsp. butter in the water and cook the turnips for about 3 minutes until they are glazed and the liquid syrupy.

TO MAKE THE SAUCE:
1 Chop the chicken bones and the carcasses, wing tips, and necks from the pigeons and fry them in some hot oil in a large heavy pan for about 10 minutes until they are brown and caramelized.
2 Add the shallots, mushrooms, garlic, thyme, and bay leaf. Cook gently for another 10 minutes. Deglaze the pan with the sherry vinegar, cooking to drive off all the liquid. Repeat with the cognac. Then add the Madeira and white wine and reduce this mixture down to a syrupy consistency.
3 Add the veal and chicken stocks and the water. Roughly chop the pigeon hearts and livers and add to the pan—they will help to clarify the stock as well as give it more flavor! Bring the sauce to a boil, skim, reduce the heat, and simmer for 20 minutes.
4 Pass the sauce through a sieve or cheesecloth several times to remove all impurities. Return the sauce to

the rinsed-out pan and boil to reduce it a little. Add a few chopped truffles. A drop or two of lemon juice or a piece of butter will also give it a lift and add sheen. Keep the sauce warm.

TO SERVE:
1 Divide the warmed lentilles between the warmed plates, making little round nests toward the bottom of the plate.
2 Place a rosti on top of each nest and then the breasts and legs of pigeon on top of that.
3 Place spoonfuls of the reserved mushroom mixture toward the top of the plate and place the ravioli on top of them. Arrange the confit of garlic on either side of it. Top the ravioli with a thin slice of truffle.
4 Place a baby navet on either side of each plate beside the pigeon breasts, with a row of button onions running down from it.
5 Spoon the sauce over the meat.

SERVES 4

"The reason why I've done two different pigeon dishes is to show how important cooking methods are. This roasted bird tastes completely different from the Pigeon

ROAST PIGEON FROM BRESSE WITH A RAVIOLI OF WILD MUSHROOMS AND A FUMET OF TRUFFLES

en Vessie. The flavors here are richer, more robust—and of

course the garnish of wild mushrooms and truffles helps bring

out that richness and robustness."

"Woodcock is the king of gamebirds. It's hard to shoot; it's beautiful; it has lots of breast and a wonderful flavor. At the restaurant we roast it with its intestines to give it more flavor, then take its breast off and split the head, so the customer can eat the brains. It's a man's dish. You can't tart around with woodcock. You have to cook it well and put it on a plate."

WOODCOCK, LENTILLES DU PAYS, WITH A RED WINE SAUCE

4 lardons of pork fat
4 woodcock, dressed but reserving
  giblets and head for garnish
  if wished
4 tbsp. clarified butter
  (see page 119)
salt and freshly ground white pepper

for the garnish:
³/₄ quantity lentilles du pays
  (see page 121)

for the sauce:
2 shallots, chopped
2 tbsp. each brunoise (very fine dice)
  of carrots and celery
3 tbsp. red wine vinegar
1 tbsp. cognac
1³/₄ cups basic red wine stock
  (see page 116)
¹/₄ oz. bittersweet chocolate

1 Preheat the oven to 450 F. Secure the lardons in place over the breast of each bird, then seal them on all sides in the hot clarified butter in a skillet or casserole over a high heat. Place each bird on a butter paper and roast, with the heads if using for garnish, in the oven for about 8–10 minutes (the flesh should still be pink). Set aside the pan with the clarified butter in it for use when making the sauce.
2 Carve off the breasts of each bird and remove the legs. Season the insides of the breasts and legs and keep them warm.

TO MAKE THE SAUCE:
1 Chop up the birds' carcasses and seal them in the pan previously set aside over a high heat. Reduce the heat and add the shallot and the brunoise of carrot and celery. Sweat until soft but not browned.
2 Deglaze the contents of the pan with the red wine vinegar and cook until almost all the liquid has gone. Do the same with the cognac. Add the red wine stock and the chopped retained livers and hearts. Bring to a boil and simmer for 5 minutes. Pass the sauce through cheesecloth.
3 Beat in the bittersweet chocolate, taste, and adjust seasoning, if necessary.

TO SERVE:
1 Make a bed of the lentilles du pays in the center of each of the 4 warmed plates and place the breasts side by side on it with the legs just below them.
2 If using, split the head across and place the two halves at the top of the plate at 2 o'clock and 10 o'clock, with the beaks radiating outward.
3 Spoon the sauce around the plate.

SERVES 4

2 tbsp. finely chopped parsley
2½ oz. chicken mousse
 (see page 120)
4 veal fillets (approx. 6 oz. each)
enough caul fat to wrap the 4 fillets
salt and freshly ground white pepper

for the sauce:
1¼ cups veal stock
 (see page 116)
few drops of heavy cream

for the garnish:
4 potato rostis (see page 121)
4 quenelles of creamed watercress
 (see page 122)
spaghetti of carrots (see page 122)
fricassee of girolle mushrooms
 (see page 122)
confit of shallots (see page 122)

1 Mix the chopped parsley into the chicken mousse, taste, and adjust the seasoning.
2 Select 4 good pieces of caul—checking each carefully to make sure it has no holes in it. Spread a little of the chicken mousse in the middle of each piece of caul and place the veal fillet on top of that. Top the fillet with a little more mousse and then wrap the caul carefully around the contents and trim off any excess.
3 Wrap the caul parcels in plastic wrap and steam them in a single layer in a steamer for about 8–10 minutes.

TO MAKE THE SAUCE:
1 Bring the veal stock to a boil and reduce it by about one-third to make about ¾ cup.
2 Tasting as you go, add a few drops of cream and seasoning.

TO SERVE:
1 Place a potato rosti in the middle of each warmed plate. Unwrap the veal fillet parcels from their plastic wrap and place them on top of the rostis.
2 Place a quenelle of watercress on the veal parcel and top this with a portion of spaghetti of carrots.
3 Arrange the fricassee of girolles and confit of shallots around the plate.
4 Spoon the sauce around, but not over, the dish.

SERVES 4

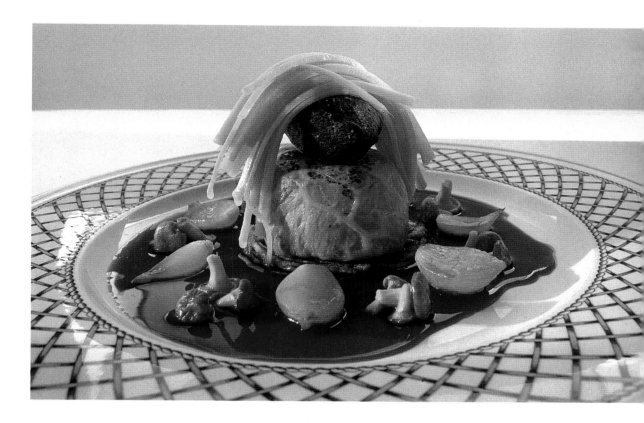

GRENADINE OF VEAL, CREAMED WATERCRESS, SPAGHETTI OF CARROTS, FRICASSEE OF GIROLLES

"I wanted this dish in the book because it was on the menu when we first opened the restaurant, and it was incredibly loyal to me, it stayed on the menu for two years. Everyone loved it. I could give it to one of my new boys. It doesn't take a great deal of skill; the hands don't have to be that disciplined."

4 slices of calf's liver, each about
 ¼ inch thick and weighing
 about 6–8 oz.
¼ cup clarified butter
salt and freshly ground white pepper
flour, for dusting

for the sauce:
2 limes
4 shallots, finely chopped
3 tbsp. butter
1 tomato, peeled, seeded, and
 coarsely chopped
1 garlic clove, split
1 tsp. sugar
½ bay leaf
2 tsp. sherry vinegar
6 tbsp. port
1¼ cups Noilly Prat
sprig of parsley
¾ cup chicken stock
1½ cups veal stock
 (see page 116)

for the garnish:
¼ cup stock syrup
 (optional, see page 123)
few drops of sherry vinegar
3 large onions, sliced
sprig of thyme
garlic clove, split
36 baby leeks, washed and trimmed

TO MAKE THE SAUCE:
1 Peel off the lime zest from one of the limes and reserve for an extra optional garnish. Segment the flesh of that lime, retaining the juices and reserving the core.
2 In a large pan over a moderate heat, sweat the shallots in a little of the butter. Add the tomato and the garlic. Sprinkle the sugar over the mixture and stir until it is dissolved. Add the bay leaf and the sherry vinegar. Cook until caramelized.

3 Deglaze the pan with the juices from the lime (also squeeze the juices from the core and then put the core into the pan). Deglaze the pan again with the port, each time cooking almost all the liquid away. Repeat with the Noilly Prat, adding the parsley at the same time and cooking off all the alcohol.
4 Add the chicken and veal stocks and boil for 10 minutes to reduce the liquid by about one-third. Pass the sauce through a sieve and then through a chinoise, or conical strainer. Bring it back to a boil and reduce by one-half.
5 Beat in the remaining butter piece by piece and incorporate it by making waves in the sauce. Check the taste and add some seasoning and some more lime juice from the second lime, if necessary. Keep warm.

TO PREPARE THE GARNISH:
1 If using, cut the lime zest into fine julienne. Blanch it and refresh it 3 times and then cover it with the stock syrup and boil to reduce the volume of syrup by half—until the zest is transparent and candied. Tasting as you go, add a few drops of sherry vinegar to give just the right sweet-and-sour taste. Set aside and keep warm.
2 Cut each lime segment into 3 and warm the pieces gently in the bottom of a small pan.
3 Sweat the onions in a little of the clarified butter, along with the thyme and the garlic, until soft. Drain off the butter and deglaze the pan with a few drops of sherry

vinegar. Cook briefly over a high heat to brown and caramelize the onions. Keep warm.
4 Blanch the leeks in a large pan of boiling water for 3 minutes. Drain thoroughly and pat dry, then glaze in a little of the melted clarified butter in a large skillet over a low heat.

TO COOK THE LIVER:
1 Preheat the oven to 450 F and lightly dust the liver in flour.
2 Heat the remaining clarified butter in a flameproof pan over a high heat (use just enough butter to cover the bottom of the pan) and fry the liver for 30 seconds on each side to seal it.
3 Remove the liver from the pan and drain off any excess fat. Place a butter paper on the bottom of the pan and replace the liver pieces on it. Cook in the oven for 2 minutes. Season with salt and pepper before serving.

TO SERVE:
1 Place piles of onion in the centers of each of the 4 warmed plates.
2 Place the liver on top of that and spoon the sauce over it. Sprinkle the lime segments over the liver, followed by the zest if using.
3 Position 9 baby leeks in a pile at the top of each plate.

SERVES 4

"This is one of the new classics; everyone does it. Liver is a rich but bland meat, and you need something sharp to cut it—like lime. Take care with the vegetables, though: lime can upset a lot of them. Leeks get on well with lime, but a

TRANCHE OF CALF'S LIVER WITH A SAUCE OF LIME

cauliflower puree, for example, would cause a lot of trouble.

It would get very offended by the lime."

2 guinea fowl, each about
   2½ lb. dressed weight
2 sprigs of thyme
2 juniper berries
3 tbsp. oil
salt and freshly ground white pepper

for the sauce:
8 shallots, finely chopped
6 oz. button mushrooms
1 garlic clove
sprig of thyme
1 dried morel
1 tbsp. cognac
¾ cup Madeira
1 cup chicken stock
2 tbsp. heavy cream
piece of butter
lemon juice to taste

for the garnish:
20 baby leeks
2 tbsp. chicken stock
½ cup butter
20 girolle mushrooms
lemon juice to taste
20 roasted button onions
   (see page 121)

1 Preheat the oven to 450 F. Chop the wings and feet off the birds and reserve for the sauce. Season the cavities of the birds with a sprig of thyme and juniper berry each and some salt and pepper.
2 Brown the birds in a little of the oil in a large pan over a high heat.
3 Cover their breasts with butter papers and roast for about 15 minutes. Let the cooked birds rest in a warm place for 5–10 minutes before carving.

TO MAKE THE SAUCE:
1 Brown the trimmings from the birds in the remaining oil in a large pan over a high heat.
2 Reduce the heat and add the shallots, mushrooms, and garlic and sweat them together until they are caramelized.
3 Add the sprig of thyme and the dried morel and then deglaze the pan with the cognac, cooking until all the liquid has been driven off. Add the Madeira and deglaze in the same way.
4 Add the chicken stock and simmer for 20 minutes. Sieve the sauce and then bring it back to a boil and beat in the cream and a piece of butter. Taste and adjust the seasoning and add a little lemon juice, if necessary. Keep warm.

TO MAKE THE GARNISH:
1 Cut off the whites of the leeks and discard the rest, apart from a few strips of green for garnish.
2 Blanch the leeks in a large pan of boiling salted water until they are tender. Refresh in cold water and cook again in the chicken stock, to which has been added a knob of butter, until the liquid has evaporated. Keep warm.
3 Cook the girolles lightly in a little butter with a dash of lemon juice. Season and keep warm.

TO SERVE:
1 Remove the legs from the birds and separate the thighs from the drumsticks. Clean the ends of the drumsticks and remove the bones from the thighs. Remove each breast in one piece. Season the meat.
2 In the middle of each of 4 warmed plates, place a thigh with a drumstick next to it. Cut the breasts across into 5 and place as a whole on top of the thigh and drumstick.
3 Pour the sauce around the guinea fowl and then sprinkle the vegetable garnishes around each plate, dressing the whites of leek with the strips of green.

SERVES 4

"This is another of our originals. It was on our first menu when we opened the restaurant, and it was on our first television program. I like this dish enormously; it's an old friend."

"A French guinea fowl is a great bird. It's cheaper than French

ROAST GUINEA FOWL WITH WILD MUSHROOMS

chicken, yet it's still got plenty of flavor. British chicken I would

never use—you're eating water. With French birds, you eat meat."

whole rib of lamb to yield
   8 double lamb chops
1 set of calf's brains
1 shallot, sliced
sprig of thyme
tiny piece of bay leaf
1½ tbsp. white wine vinegar
8 tsp. chicken mousse
   (see page 120)
2 tbsp. chopped tarragon
24 whole tarragon leaves for
   decoration
caul fat to cover the meat
clarified butter, to seal (see page 119)
salt and freshly ground white pepper

for the jus of tarragon:
1 chicken leg (optional)
½ onion, diced small
2 carrots, diced small
½ stick of celery, diced small
3 tbsp. olive oil
1 large garlic clove, split
2 tbsp. brandy
¾ cup dry white wine
3½ cups veal stock
   (see page 116)
1¾ cups chicken stock
sprig of thyme
sprig of tarragon
tiny piece of bay leaf
5 white peppercorns
4 tarragon leaves
4 tomatoes, seeded and diced

for the garnish:
fettuccine of vegetables
   (see page 120)

1 Get the butcher to do the following, or do it yourself: remove the chine bone from the rib, strip off the back fat, and cut the joint into the 8 chops each having two bones. For each chop, one bone should be cut off and the other trimmed to about 2 inches in length and scraped clean of fat. Finally, the rather thick chops should be flattened slightly with the flat side of a meat cleaver or knife. Keep the trimmings and put the chops in the refrigerator to set.
2 Soak the brains in cold water for about 2 hours to blanch out the blood. Being very careful with the very delicate flesh, separate the brains down the middle. Place one half in the palm of the hand with the severed side uppermost. Gently stroke off the membrane that surrounds the brain. Do this slowly and exactingly, do not rush the process! Repeat with the other half.

3 Rinse the brains again and then place in a pan with just enough cold water to cover. Add the shallot, thyme, bay leaf, vinegar, and salt and bring to just *below* a boil. Lower the heat and simmer very gently for about 10 minutes. Remove from the heat and allow the brains to cool in the liquid. Once cool, drain and put in the refrigerator to set.
4 After 30 minutes or so, cut the brains into eight ¼ inch thick slices. Mix the chicken mousse with the tarragon. Spread a little of this mixture on each chop and top with a slice of brains. Top this with 3 whole tarragon leaves for decoration. Season these covered chops well and then wrap each in caul fat—ensuring that there are no holes in the caul. Twist the caul under the chop to seal it and cut off any excess. Refrigerate until needed.

FOR THE SAUCE:
1 Preheat the oven to 425 F and then roast the lamb bones, with the chicken leg—if using, for extra flavor—until they are brown.
2 In a large pan over a moderate heat, sweat the diced vegetables in a little oil with the garlic. Cook until the mixture is just beginning to become caramelized.
3 Add the roasted bones, and chicken if using, to the pan of vegetables and deglaze the contents of the pan with the brandy. Add the white wine and boil to reduce away completely. Pour in enough of the stocks (in a proportion of 2:1 veal stock to chicken stock) to cover the bones. Add the sprigs of thyme, tarragon, bay leaf, and peppercorns. Bring to a boil and simmer for 35 minutes.
4 When the sauce is ready, pass it through a fine sieve several times and then return it to the pan.

Boil rapidly to reduce the volume by about one-third. Add the tarragon leaves and allow to infuse for 15 seconds. Add the diced tomatoes and allow to infuse for an additional 10 seconds. Taste and adjust the seasoning, if necessary. Keep warm.

TO SERVE:
1 Very gently seal the caul-wrapped chops in hot clarified butter in a large pan and then wrap them in plastic wrap and steam in a single layer in a steamer for 5 minutes.
2 Unwrap the chops and place them, in pairs with their trimmed bones crossed, on each warm plate.
3 Twist the vegetable fettuccine into 4 balls and place one at the top of each plate.
4 Spoon the sauce around the plate.

SERVES 4

"When I first opened Harvey's, I had a phase during which I went mad on pasta. Tagliatelle of this, tortelloni of that, fettuccine of vegetables ... the Italian influence, again.

NOISETTES OF LAMB EN CREPINETTE, FETTUCCINE OF VEGETABLES, JUS OF TARRAGON

Simple things, good-looking things. Texture and flavor.

That's the base of everything."

4 plump pigeons, dressed
8 sprigs of thyme
4 juniper berries
1 tbsp. brandy
1 tbsp. port
1 tbsp. Madeira
salt and freshly ground white pepper

for the sauce:
¼ cup clarified butter
  (see page 119)
mirepoix (cut into ¼ inch dice) of:
  2 tbsp. shallots, 1 tbsp. carrot,
  1 tbsp. celery
3 garlic cloves, split across in half
7 sprigs of thyme
2 white peppercorns, crushed
1 tbsp. cognac
6 tbsp. dry white wine
1¼ cups veal stock
  (see page 116)
⅔ cup chicken stock
⅔ cup water
1 tbsp. tomato paste
¼ bay leaf
2 tsp. cream

for the garnish:
10 very small baby leeks
goose fat, for frying
4 balls of tagliatelle
  (see page 119)
piece of butter
8 thin slices of truffle
40 roasted button onions
  (see page 121)
confit of garlic (see page 122)

1 Trim the pigeons' wing tips, remove any remaining feathers and clean their cavities.
2 Place a sprig of thyme between the skin and breast flesh on either side of the breast bone on each bird. Season inside the cavity with salt and pepper and add one juniper berry to each cavity.

3 Put each bird in a pig's bladder (or roasting bag) and add along with it equal amounts of the brandy, port, and Madeira. Expel as much air as possible from the bladder before tying it very securely with string.
4 Place the bladders in a large pan filled with boiling water and simmer for 17 minutes. Take them out of the saucepan and let the pigeons rest in their bladders for a good 5 minutes.
5 Take the birds out of their bladders, carve the legs and breast of each of them, cover the cooked flesh with plastic wrap, and keep warm.

TO MAKE THE SAUCE:
1 Chop up the pigeon carcasses and brown them lightly in the clarified butter in a large pan over a moderate heat.
2 Add the vegetable mirepoix, 1 split garlic clove, 1 sprig of thyme, and the 2 crushed

peppercorns. Continue to cook until these are lightly browned then deglaze the pan with the cognac. When the alcohol has been driven off, add the white wine and then boil to reduce this by half.
3 Add the chicken stock, water, veal stock, tomato paste, bay leaf, 4 sprigs of thyme, and the remaining garlic. Bring the mixture to a boil and skim and simmer for about 10 minutes.
4 Pass the sauce through a sieve several times, then bring it back to a boil and reduce it by half (you should have about 1¾ cups). Add the 2 remaining sprigs of thyme and beat in the cream. Keep warm.

TO MAKE THE GARNISH:
1 Cut the leeks into 1 inch lengths (you should get at least 2 from each leek) and cook them in a little goose fat in a large skillet over a moderate heat for about 2½ minutes. Drain. Season with salt and keep warm.

2 Just before serving, warm the tagliatelle through in an emulsion of butter in just enough water to cover and then form into 4 balls as described on page 119.

TO SERVE:
1 Place the pigeon breasts side by side in the center of each of the 4 warmed plates, with the legs just below them.
2 Place a ball of tagliatelle at the top of each plate with 5 of the leek pieces perched on top of each ball in a lattice effect. Top this with a couple of truffle slices.
3 Arrange the button onions around the bottom of each plate, with the confit of garlic in piles at 4 o'clock and 7 o'clock on each plate.
4 Spoon the sauce over the meat and around the plate.

SERVES 4

"This is pigeon cooked in a pig's bladder. You can cook a pigeon in different ways, but unless it's a fleshy bird it needs some sort of protection, and the bladder protects it. When you drop it in the water the bladder blows up like a balloon, so the bird is steamed with It's a very gentle way of cooking a pigeon;

PIGEON EN VESSIE WITH A TAGLIATELLE OF LEEKS AND TRUFFLES, JUS OF THYME

thyme sprigs in a mixture of port, madeira, and brandy vapors.

it keeps it moist and delicate."

"**When people are judging a dish, they look at the meat, not the vegetables. Good meat is crucial to any restaurant, and particularly good beef. The Brits love their beef. A man orders this dish, and he wants a plate of beef, not two silly little slices. It's a great dish with a great flavor.**"

4 x 10 oz. rib eyes of Scotch beef
2 tbsp. clarified butter
   (see page 119)
salt and freshly ground white pepper

for the sauce:
10 shallots, chopped
1¾ cups red wine
sprig of thyme
½ bay leaf
3 tbsp. port
3 tbsp. red wine vinegar
1¼ cups veal stock
   (see page 116)
6 tbsp. chicken stock
1 tbsp. butter

for the garnish:
confit of garlic (see page 122)
confit of shallots (see page 122)
fricassee of mushrooms
   (see page 122)
4 quenelles of creamed parsley
   (see page 122)

TO MAKE THE SAUCE:
1 Mix together the shallots, red wine, thyme, bay leaf, port, and red wine vinegar. Allow to infuse overnight.
2 Bring to a boil and reduce by two-thirds. Remove the thyme and bay leaf. Add the veal and chicken stock, bring back to a boil, and reduce by half.
3 Add the butter and make waves in the saucepan to incorporate it. Check the taste and adjust the seasoning, if necessary.

TO COOK THE BEEF:
1 Season the beef well with salt and pepper on each side.
2 In a large skillet heat the clarified butter over a high heat until almost smoking and sauté the beef on each side until it is cooked medium-rare.

TO SERVE:
1 Cut each piece of beef into 12 slices and fan these around the middle of each of 4 warmed plates. Place a small heap of confit of garlic on one side of the beef and shallots on the other.
2 Place the mushroom fricassee in lines around the remaining edges of the plate.
3 Spoon the sauce over the meat and around the plate.
4 Top the beef with a quenelle of creamed parsley.

SERVES 4

PIECE OF SCOTCH BEEF, CONFIT OF SHALLOTS AND GARLIC WITH A RED WINE AND SHALLOT SAUCE

1 cup hazelnuts
1²/₃ cups superfine sugar
6 egg whites
1½ cups heavy cream
oil, for greasing

for the almond praline pyramids:
¾ cup slivered almonds
12 oz. fondant with 3 tbsp. water
   or
   1½ cups superfine sugar
   2 tbsp. liquid glucose
   6 tbsp. water

for the passion fruit coulis:
1 cup passion fruit pulp
   (about 12 fruit)
2 tbsp. superfine sugar
1 tbsp. water
3 tbsp. fresh orange juice
5 tbsp. stock syrup
   (see page 123)

for the garnish:
40 orange segments, peeled and
   chopped
40 pink grapefruit segments, peeled
   and chopped
julienne of orange and lemon zest
   (see page 125)
60 tiny double mint leaves

1 Preheat the oven to 450 F.
Place the hazelnuts on a baking
sheet and roast them in the oven
for 5 minutes.
2 Rub off the skins from the
roasted hazelnuts (otherwise the
praline will be bitter). Smash the
skinned nuts with a rolling pin
until they are roughly about one-
quarter their original size.
3 Put ½ cup of the sugar in a
heavy pan over a medium to high
heat. Add the hazelnuts, but don't
stir as the sugar will then harden
around the nuts—just prod the
mixture as it starts melting after
about 3 minutes of cooking.
4 When the mixture is bubbling,
tip it out on a well-oiled heat-
proof surface and allow to set.
When cool, crush it with the end
of a rolling pin into small coarse
chunks of praline about the size
of the original smashed nuts—
not powder!
5 Beat the egg whites until frothy
and then add one-quarter of the
remaining sugar. Continue beating,
adding the rest of the sugar
gradually until it is all incorporated
and the meringue is standing in
soft peaks.
6 In a separate bowl, beat the
cream until thickened but not
stiff. Fold the cream gently into
the meringue followed by the
praline chunks.
7 Line a 12 × 3 inch terrine or
loaf pan with plastic wrap, leaving
a generous overhang all around.
Spoon the mixture into the terrine,
tapping it from time to time to get
rid of air pockets. Bring up the
overhanging plastic wrap to wrap
it. Freeze for at least 6 hours.

TO MAKE THE ALMOND
PRALINE PYRAMIDS:
1 Roast the almonds in the
hot oven for about 3–5 minutes,
watching them closely in the
last minutes to ensure that they
do not burn.
2 Put the fondant with 3 tbsp.
water—or the sugar, glucose,
and 4 tbsp. water—into a heavy
saucepan and boil to hard crack
stage (see Sugar cage, page 124):
the mixture should then be a
light golden color and in the
temperature range 295–320 F.
3 Stir the almonds in gently,
then pour the mixture out on
an oiled slab or parchment paper
to harden and cool.
4 When quite cool and hard,
break up into pieces with a rolling
pin and grind to a fine powder
in a blender.
5 Preheat the oven to 350 F.
Sprinkle the powder evenly
to a depth of about ¼ inch
over an oiled baking sheet
and melt the powder in the
oven until it is a good brown
color. Allow it to cool slightly
and then cut the praline into
30 triangles (4 × 4 × 3 inches)
and place on a nonstick surface
to harden fully. (If the praline
hardens while cutting, simply
return it to the oven briefly
to make it pliable again.) Use
immediately, or store in an
airtight container until required.

TO MAKE THE PASSION
FRUIT COULIS:
1 Put the passion fruit pulp and
seeds in a saucepan with the
superfine sugar and water. Bring
the mixture to a boil and simmer
for 2–3 minutes. Blend the mixture
and sieve it.
2 Add the orange juice and stock
syrup to the sieved pulp and bring
to a boil. Skim carefully, sieve, and
allow to cool.

TO SERVE:
1 Cut the block of frozen nougat
into 10 pyramids with sides
the dimensions of the almond
praline triangles.
2 Pour the coulis on 10 chilled
plates and place a pyramid in the
center of that.
3 Press the praline triangles on
each of the sides of the pyramid
to form an outer casing.
4 Sprinkle the pieces of orange
and pink grapefruit segments
alternately around the edge of the
plate and garnish with candied zest
of oranges and lemons and tiny
mint leaves.

SERVES 10

"I love nougat. In Italy, we had nougat instead of Easter eggs when we were children—great big blocks of it, coated in rice paper and then wrapped in cotton cloth or in foil. This is a frozen nougatine which is quite incredible, smooth, yet with great crunch. The sharpness of the

BISCUIT GLACÉ

passion fruit helps cut the sweetness of the nougatine.”

4 cups red currants
²/₃ cup superfine sugar
juice of ½ lemon
1 tbsp. Mirabelle liqueur
80 fresh raspberries
5 tbsp. raspberry coulis
   (see page 124)
4 pâtes tulipe (see page 124)
4 sugar cages (optional,
   see page 124)
julienne of orange zest
   (see page 125)
24 tiny mint leaves

for the sabayon sauce:
3 egg yolks
¼ cup superfine sugar
6 tbsp. champagne

1 Blend the red currants, reserving a few for garnish, with the superfine sugar, lemon juice, and liqueur. Taste and add more lemon juice if necessary.
2 Sieve and freeze into a sorbet in an ice-cream maker.
3 Just before serving, toss the reserved red currants and the raspberries in a little of the raspberry coulis.

TO MAKE THE SABAYON SAUCE:
1 Mix the egg yolks with the superfine sugar and champagne.
2 Beat the mixture in a double boiler, or bowl set over a saucepan of hot water, for about 3 minutes until it is creamy and frothy.

TO SERVE:
1 Preheat a very hot broiler. Make 5 little circles of coulis around each of 4 large chilled serving plates. Arrange a pyramid of raspberries on each circle (4 per pyramid).
2 Spoon a little sabayon over the raspberries and then flash the plates under the broiler briefly to brown the sauce.
3 Place a pâte tulipe in the middle of each plate with a ball of red currant sorbet in the center of that. If you wish, you can put a decorative sugar cage over the sorbet.
4 Garnish with a little zest of orange, some mint leaves, and the reserved red currants dressed in the coulis.

SERVES 4

"The English love red fruit, don't they? They'd love to have strawberries and cream at Harvey's, served on grand trays, in silver bowls, with cream in a tall silver pitcher and an antique sugar shaker to hand—but I haven't the room or the time or the staff for all that. So I take a mixture of red fruits

GRATIN OF RED FRUITS

and glaze them in a red fruit sauce, then put them in the oven to

warm them through, like the sun, then I cover them in this white,

soufflé-like sauce. It's the nearest I can get to serving

strawberries and cream."

9 mangoes
8½ oz. puff pastry
2 tbsp. superfine sugar

for the pineapple sorbet:
1 lb. 2 oz. fresh pineapple,
   peeled and cored
1 cup superfine sugar
1 cup stock syrup
   (see page 123)
juice of ¼ lemon

for the mango glaze:
¾ cup superfine sugar
4 tbsp. stock syrup
   (see page 123)
4 tbsp. Bacardi rum
4½ tbsp. unsalted butter

TO MAKE THE PINEAPPLE SORBET:
1 Blend the pineapple in a blender
or food processor and sieve it.
2 Add the sugar and stock syrup
and blend again. Add lemon juice
to taste.
3 Freeze in an ice-cream maker.

TO MAKE THE MANGO GLAZE:
1 Peel 3 of the mangoes, chop
their flesh finely, and put it with
their pits, the sugar, and stock syrup
in a saucepan and place over a
moderate heat.
2 As the mixture warms up, add
the water. Then bring to a boil
and reduce by half.
3 Take the mixture off the heat
and add the Bacardi and butter.
Place back on a gentle heat and
stir to mix until warmed through
again. Sieve the mixture before use.

TO MAKE THE TARTS:
1 Preheat the oven to 375 F.
Roll the pastry out to barely
⅛ inch thick and 16 inches

square. Cut out four 7 inch circles
(average tea-plate size). Allow to
rest for 20 minutes.
2 Peel the remaining mangoes
carefully and then cut each peeled
mango lengthwise into 3 lobes.
Put these to one side.
3 Trim off all the flesh from
around the pits, cut into small dice,
and place in the centers of the
pastry circles to add height to
the arrangement.
4 Lay each mango lobe flat and
cut it into ½ inch slices, making
half-moon segments. Arrange
these half-moons in overlapping
fans around the pastry circles
(leaving a ¼ inch clear edge all
around). The dish should now
resemble classic tartes *aux pommes*.
Save the last few segments to
arrange around the space at the

center of the circles. If the mangoes
slither around too much to arrange
with ease, use a little superfine
sugar to secure them.
5 Sprinkle the whole tarts with
a little superfine sugar and cook
in the oven for 8–10 minutes.
5 and 8 minutes into cooking
and just before serving, moisten
the top of the tarts with the
mango glaze.

TO SERVE:
1 After the final glazing of the
tarts, place them on 4 warmed
serving plates.
2 Place a quenelle of the pineapple
sorbet on top of each.
3 Spoon a little of the glaze around
the plates.

SERVES 4

"I'm playing with classics, again—this was

what happened when I started to think

about Tarte Tatin. I kept the upside-

down bit, because it's such a brilliant idea;

apples sent me off to pineapples, and from pineapples

it was only a short step to mangoes. The combination

HOT MANGO TART

works well, both in flavor terms and in textures—the crisp

tart and the creamy sorbet, the hot and the cold."

LEMON TART

4½ cups all-purpose flour
½ cup confectioners' sugar
1 cup butter, diced
grated zest of 1 lemon
seeds from 1 vanilla bean
1½ eggs
½ cup sifted confectioners' sugar,
    to dust
flour, for dusting
butter, for greasing

for the lemon filling:
9 eggs
1¾ cups superfine sugar
5 lemons (zest of 2 and juice of all 5)
1 cup heavy cream

TO MAKE THE TART SHELL:
1 Preheat the oven to 350 F. Sift the flour and confectioners' sugar and work in the butter.
2 Make a well in the flour mixture and add the lemon zest and vanilla seeds.
3 Beat the eggs and add to the well. Knead the mixture with the fingers, then wrap in plastic wrap and allow to rest for 30 minutes in the refrigerator.
4 Roll out the pastry on a lightly floured surface to a size just large enough to fill the tart pan or ring to be used.
5 Using either a greased tart ring on a greased baking sheet, or a greased tart pan with a removable base, fold the dough into it. Gently ease the dough into the corners of the tin, ensuring a good ½ inch overhang. Do not cut this off.
6 Line the tart with waxed paper and fill with enough dry pie weights or lentils to ensure that the sides as well as the base are weighted. This helps give a good finished tart shape.
7 Bake in the oven for 10 minutes. After 10 minutes, remove the weights and waxed paper and trim the overhang from the tart. Return the tart to the oven for an additional 10 minutes.

TO MAKE THE LEMON FILLING:
1 Beat the eggs with the sugar and the lemon zest.
2 Stir in the lemon juice and then fold in the cream. Remove any froth from the top of the mixture.

TO MAKE THE FLAN:
1 Reduce the oven temperature to 250 F.
2 Pour the cold filling into the hot pastry (this ensures that the pastry shell will be sealed and hold the filling) and bake for 30 minutes in the oven.

TO SERVE:
1 Preheat a very hot broiler.
2 Sift the confectioners' sugar over the tart as soon as it comes out of the oven and then flash it briefly under the broiler to caramelize the sugar.
3 Cut into 8 slices.

SERVES 8

"If I went to the Gavroche, I'd order lemon tart. It's one of my great favorites—a wonderful way of finishing a meal, and a real chef's pudding. Any chef worthy of the name has a lemon tart on his menu. We cook one twice a day: in the morning just before lunch service, and at 7 P.M. just before the dinner service, so it's always fresh and fragrant."

"Passion fruit has a persistent flavor: eat it, and you've still got the flavor in your mouth five minutes later. That's exactly what you need for a soufflé: something sharpish and long to match the sweet, eggy blandness."

"A soufflé needs heart. A lot of people go crazy trying to make them as light as possible, but you end up losing texture and substance. A good soufflé has an inside and an outside—and a middle, a heart."

50 passion fruit
4 tbsp. water

for the passion fruit sorbet:
¾ cup fresh orange juice
  (2 or 3 oranges)
6 tbsp. stock syrup
  (see page 123)

for the soufflés:
4 tbsp. crème pâtissière
  (see page 123)
10 egg whites
⅓ cup superfine sugar
few drops of lemon juice
clarified butter, to grease soufflé
  dishes (see page 119)
sugar, to line soufflé dishes and
  for dusting

1 Cut all 50 passion fruit in half and scrape out the seeds and juice into a pan. Cook gently with the water for about 5 minutes over a low heat.
2 Blend the mixture for 30 seconds (avoid pulverizing completely or the seeds will discolor the mixture!). Rub the mixture through a sieve 2 or 3 times. Divide the mixture into 2 halves.

TO MAKE THE PASSION FRUIT SORBET:
1 Add the orange juice and stock syrup to half the sieved passion fruit pulp. Check the

taste and adjust with a little sugar, if necessary.
2 Freeze in an ice-cream maker.

TO MAKE THE SOUFFLÉS:
1 Preheat the oven to 350 F. Bring the other half of the sieved pulp slowly up to a boil and reduce the volume by about half, producing about ¼ cup. Allow to cool.
2 Beat the cooled mixture with the crème pâtissière. Then beat the egg whites until frothy and gradually add the sugar to it in small batches until it has all been incorporated. Beat to a soft peak and then beat in the lemon juice.
3 Grease 4 small soufflé dishes with the butter and sprinkle them with a fine coating of sugar. Tap out any excess.
4 Fold the meringue mixture gently into the passion fruit mixture and spoon this into the lined soufflé dishes. Make sure that the very top both inside and outside the dish is absolutely free of mixture or it will stick and fail to rise evenly on cooking.
5 Place the soufflé dishes on a baking sheet and cook in the oven for 7 minutes until well risen and golden brown on top. Remove from the oven, dust with confectioners' sugar, and serve immediately accompanied by the sorbet.

SERVES 4

PASSION FRUIT SOUFFLÉS

6 large pears
juice of 3 lemons
4½ cups water
2¼ cups superfine sugar
superfine sugar, for sprinkling

for the honey ice cream:
6 egg yolks
⅓ cup superfine sugar
2 cups milk
6 tbsp. heavy cream
½ cup honey

for the caramel sauce:
½ cup superfine sugar with
   6 tbsp. water
   or
   6 tbsp. poaching liquid
   from cooking the pears
6 tbsp. Poire William liqueur
lemon juice to taste

for the garnish:
4 tuile baskets (see page 124)
julienne of lemon and orange zest
   (see page 125)
24 red currants
4 tiny mint leaves
sifted confectioners' sugar, to dust

TO MAKE THE ICE CREAM:
1 Beat together the egg yolks
and the sugar.

2 Bring the milk to a boil in a
saucepan and pour it over the egg
and sugar mixture. Return to the
heat and stir constantly until the
mixture has thickened to a custard.
3 Take off the heat and stir in the
heavy cream and honey.
4 Leave until cold and then freeze
in an ice-cream maker.

TO POACH THE PEARS:
1 Peel the pears and reserve the
skins. Put the freshly peeled pears
in enough water to cover with a
little lemon juice to prevent them
from discoloring.
2 Cut a circle of waxed paper to
fit a large saucepan in which the
pears will be poached. In this pan,
stir the sugar into the 4½ cups
water and bring the mixture to a
boil. Add the lemon juice and then
5 of the pears. Cover the surface of
the liquid with the paper and bring
the mixture back to a boil as fast
as possible.
3 Simmer gently for 5 minutes,
then check to see if the pears are
done by piercing them with a
knife. When done, remove the pan
from the heat but allow the pears
to cool in the liquid.
4 When they are cool, drain
thoroughly and put to one side.

5 Using a small ball cutter (melon
baller), from the remaining whole
uncooked pear scoop out as many
balls of pear flesh as possible.
6 Put the pear balls in the cooled
poaching syrup. Gently bring the
mixture to a boil, then remove
from the heat and allow the balls to
cool in the syrup. Drain before use.

TO MAKE THE CARAMEL SAUCE:
1 In a skillet over a low heat
gently fry the pear skins with the
sugar. They should eventually
become caramelized.
2 Add the water and sugar mixture,
or the poaching syrup, and bring to
a boil. Simmer for 5 minutes.
3 Sieve the sauce and then add the
Poire William liqueur and a drop or
two of lemon juice to taste.

TO SERVE:
1 Preheat a very hot broiler.
2 Slice each whole poached pear
downward from the stalk to get
3 good flat oval slices from each
side of the core. Place the pear
slices on a baking sheet and
sprinkle them liberally with
superfine sugar. Place them under
a hot broiler to caramelize the
sugar and give the pear slices a
crunchy candied surface.

3 Place these pear slices around
the edges of the serving plates. Cut
more slices from around the cores
of the pear and arrange these in
star shapes in the middle of each
plate. Place the tuile basket in the
middle of each star. Fill the basket
with honey ice cream and spoon
the caramel sauce between the pear
"stepping stones."
4 Garnish each dish with julienne
of lemon and orange zest, red
currants dusted with confectioners'
sugar, the pear balls, and the tiny
mint leaves.

SERVES 4

"We use a blowtorch to caramelize the poached pears—it gives them a great texture, like eating candied apples. When we started Harvey's, we were skint, we couldn't even afford a broiler. So we played around with a blowtorch

ROASTED PEARS WITH HONEY ICE CREAM

for gratins and glazes, and it worked really well."

4 peaches, about three-quarters ripe
4 cups superfine sugar
4½ cups water
1 vanilla bean
sifted confectioners' sugar, to dust

for the marzipan mold:
1½ cups confectioners' sugar
1 tbsp. cornstarch
1⅓ cups ground almonds
2 egg whites

for the vanilla ice cream:
1 or 2 vanilla beans
2 cups milk
6 egg yolks
1 cup superfine sugar
2½ cups heavy cream

for the garnish:
raspberry coulis (see page 124)
4 sugar cages (see page 124)
candied nuts (see page 125)
red currants, white currants, and
    fraises du bois
mint leaves

TO MAKE THE MARZIPAN MOLD:
1 Mix all the ingredients together
thoroughly into a smooth dough.
Wrap this dough in plastic wrap
and allow it to rest for an hour
or so.
2 On a surface lightly dusted
with sifted confectioners' sugar, roll
out the marzipan dough until it is
super thin. Cut into four 4½ inch
diameter circles and press these into
small nonstick pastry, muffin, or
Yorkshire pudding molds of the
same size.
3 Allow the marzipan to dry,
preferably overnight, in a dry but
airy place. Then remove them from
their molds.
4 Just before serving, flash the
marzipan shells under a very hot
broiler to brown them.

TO MAKE THE VANILLA ICE CREAM:
1 Split the vanilla beans
lengthwise, put these in the
milk in a saucepan and bring
it to a boil.
2 Beat the egg yolks and sugar
together thoroughly and pour the
boiling milk onto that mixture,
stirring all the time. Return to the
saucepan and cook, again stirring
continuously, until the mixture
coats the back of a spoon.
3 Away from the heat, incorporate
the cream and allow the mixture to
cool. When cool, put to freeze in
an ice-cream maker.

TO POACH THE PEACHES:
1 Cut a circle of waxed paper to
fit the pan in which you will be
poaching the peaches.
2 Dissolve the sugar in the water,
add the vanilla bean, and bring to
a boil slowly. When the mixture is
boiling add the peaches and cover
with the paper. Bring back to a
boil as quickly as possible and then
reduce the heat and simmer gently
for about 5 minutes.
3 Test the peaches with the point
of a knife to see if they are done.
When tender but still firm, remove
from the heat and allow to cool in
the poaching liquid.

TO SERVE:
1 Smooth the raspberry coulis over
the center of each of 4 plates. Fill
the browned marzipan molds with
a smooth slab of vanilla ice cream
and place them in the middle of
the pool of coulis.
2 Top the ice cream with a peach
and a sugar cage and garnish
with candied nuts and some of
the red currants, white currants,
and fraises du bois which have
been dusted with a little of the
sifted confectioners' sugar. Top
with mint leaves.

SERVES 4

"This is an Escoffier classic,
of course. Escoffier sprinkled
almonds on the top, so I
replaced the almonds with a
basket made of fresh
marzipan and dried it with a blowtorch to get
it really golden. That's my
interpretation; but the
original combination of
raspberries and ice cream

PEACH MELBA

and peaches is permanent, wonderful."

2 tbsp. milk, warmed
¼ oz. yeast
1 cup all-purpose flour
½ cup superfine sugar
1½ eggs
pinch of salt
¼ cup butter, melted
1 cup water
2 tbsp. mirabelle liqueur
oil, for greasing
flour, for dusting

for the mirabelle glaze:
1 lb. 2 oz. mirabelles
1 cup superfine sugar
1¼ cups water

for the sabayon sauce:
3 egg yolks
¼ cup superfine sugar
6 tbsp. Kirsch
1 tbsp. stock syrup
  (see page 123)
6 tbsp. heavy cream,
  whipped to soft peaks

for the garnish:
3⅓ cups fresh raspberries
2 tbsp. raspberry coulis
  (see page 124)
about 48 red currants
about 48 white currants
sifted confectioners' sugar, to dust
tiny mint leaves

1 Mix the warm milk with the yeast and 1 tbsp. of the flour to start the fermentation. When the process has started and the mixture is foaming, add the remaining flour, ½ tbsp. sugar, the eggs, and the salt. Mix to a dough.

2 Make an indentation in the top of the dough and pour the melted butter into it. Cover the dough with a cloth and allow to rise in a warm place until it has roughly doubled in volume.

3 Knead the dough until all the butter has been absorbed and then use the dough to half fill four 3½ inch greased and floured savarin (rum baba) molds. Again leave to rise in a warm place until they have doubled in size. Preheat the oven to 425 F.

4 Bake the risen savarins in the oven for about 15 minutes. Turn out on a cooling rack and allow to cool.

5 Heat the remaining sugar, water, and mirabelle liqueur in a saucepan until the sugar is dissolved. Using a slotted spoon, dip each cooled savarin into the hot syrup until they are thoroughly soaked with it. Allow to drain on a cooling rack.

TO MAKE THE MIRABELLE GLAZE:

1 Put the mirabelles, sugar, and water in a saucepan and bring to a boil. Simmer gently for about 5 minutes. Then blend the contents of the pan and pass through a sieve.

2 Return the sieved mixture to the pan and bring to a boil.

Continue to boil until it is reduced by about one-third. It should now have the syrupy consistency of a light glaze.

3 Using a pastry brush, glaze the savarins with the syrup.

TO MAKE THE SAUCE:

1 Mix the egg yolks with the superfine sugar, Kirsch, and stock syrup and then beat the mixture in a double boiler over a gentle heat for about 5 minutes, until the mixture is frothy and creamy.

2 Remove from the heat and continue to beat until the mixture is cool. When cool, fold in the heavy cream.

TO SERVE:

1 Macerate the raspberries in the coulis, just long enough to coat them without softening the flesh, and dust the red currants and white currants in a little sifted confectioners' sugar.

2 Make a circle of cold sabayon sauce in the center of each plate and place the savarin in the center of that.

3 Build up the raspberries in the savarin to a pyramid shape.

4 Arrange 3 piles of 4 or 5 each of the white currants and red currants on each plate.

5 Top the pyramid of raspberries and each pile of fruit with mint leaves.

SERVES 4

"This is my version of rum baba. I never liked rum baba until, on the 'Take Six Cooks' television series, I had to eat one that Robert Mey of the Carlton Tower had prepared. 'I don't like this,' I thought, 'but I'd better eat some for the camera.' It was absolutely delicious, served with an apricot coulis

SAVARIN OF RASPBERRIES

to relieve the sweetness. I use raspberries in a similar way."

for the white chocolate sorbet:
6 oz. white chocolate
2/3 cup Noilly Prat
1 tbsp. vodka
2 1/3 cups water
3/4 cup stock syrup (see page 123)
grated fresh zest of 1 orange

for the dark chocolate mousse:
4 oz. bittersweet chocolate
2 tbsp. unsalted butter, melted
1 cup heavy cream
6 egg whites
2 tbsp. superfine sugar
1 tbsp. Grand Marnier (optional)

for the raspberry mousse:
1 1/4 cups fresh raspberries
3 tbsp. water
2 tbsp. superfine sugar
1 1/4 leaves gelatin
1 tbsp. framboise liqueur (optional)
6 egg whites
1 cup heavy cream

**for the chocolate sauce and
   sheeting:**
4 oz. semisweet chocolate
2 oz. white chocolate

for the hot chocolate soufflé:
1/4 cup cocoa powder
2 tbsp. water
3 egg yolks
1 tsp. Cointreau (optional)
4 egg whites
1 tsp. superfine sugar
clarified butter, to grease molds
   (see page 119)
superfine sugar, to line molds

for the garnish:
julienne of orange zest
   (see page 125)
12 tiny mint leaves
16 raspberries
confectioners' sugar, to dust

TO MAKE THE WHITE CHOCOLATE
SORBET:
1 Break the chocolate into pieces
and place in a saucepan with the
Noilly Prat and vodka. Heat
through—but do not boil.
2 Once the chocolate has all
melted, add the water and bring
the mixture to a boil.
3 Remove from the heat and add
the stock syrup and grated orange
zest. Allow to cool then freeze in
an ice-cream maker.

TO MAKE THE DARK CHOCOLATE
MOUSSE:
1 Prepare a small tray (about
7 × 3½ inches and about ½ inch
deep) by lining it with plastic
wrap, leaving a good overhang.
2 Melt the chocolate in a saucepan
and add the softened butter.
3 Whip the cream until firm but
not too stiff.
4 Beat the egg whites to soft
peaks, incorporating the sugar
about halfway through the process.
5 Take the chocolate off the heat
and gently fold the egg whites into
it, followed by the cream. Lightly
flavor the mixture with the liqueur,
if using, and allow to cool a little.
6 Spread the mixture into the
prepared tray, cover with the plastic
wrap overhang, and put in the
refrigerator to firm it up.

TO MAKE THE RASPBERRY MOUSSE:
1 Bring the raspberries, water,
and 1 tbsp. sugar to a boil in a
saucepan and reduce by one-
third. Pass through a sieve.

2 Soften the gelatin in a little cold
water and then work it into the
raspberry puree. Add the liqueur,
if using.
3 Beat the egg whites and
remaining sugar to make a
meringue. Whip the cream to
soft peaks and fold the meringue
into the fruit pulp, followed by
the cream.
4 Spread the mixture on a
plastic-wrap-lined tray (as for
the chocolate mousse) and store
in the refrigerator until set.

TO MAKE THE CHOCOLATE SAUCE
AND SHEETING:
1 Cut the 2 sides of a plastic sack
to the size of baking sheets.
2 Sprinkle a few drops of water
on 2 baking sheets and then place
the plastic sheets on top of them
(the water prevents the plastic
from slipping).
3 Melt the chocolates gently in
2 separate pans and then paint each
plastic sheet with one type of
chocolate. It should be no more
than 1/16 inch thick. Leave the
sheets in the refrigerator to set.
4 Using a circular pastry cutter,
about 2 inches in diameter, cut out
8 circles of dark chocolate. Then
using another smaller circular pastry
cutter, about 1¾ inches in diameter,
very carefully cut the centers out of
these circles to make 8 rings and
8 smaller dark chocolate circles.
5 From both the dark and the
white chocolate, cut out rectangles
about 7 × 3½ inches. Then cut
these across in half and then cut

those halves diagonally across in
half again to make 4 triangles of
each color.
6 Melt what is left of the dark
chocolate back in its pan to make
a sauce.

TO MAKE THE HOT CHOCOLATE
SOUFFLÉ:
1 Preheat the oven to 350 F.
Grease 4 small dariole molds or
ramekins (or ovenproof egg cups
as used here) with clarified butter
and then line them with a dusting
of superfine sugar.
2 Make a paste of the cocoa
powder and water and add the egg
yolks and the Cointreau, if using.
3 Beat the egg whites to firm
peaks, incorporating the sugar
halfway through. Fold this into
the chocolate mixture.
4 Spoon the mixture into the
prepared molds and bake in the
oven for about 4 or 5 minutes
until well risen and set. Serve
immediately, dusted with
confectioners' sugar.

TO SERVE:
1 On each of 4 large dinner
plates place 3 small pools of dark
chocolate sauce at equal intervals
around the edge.
2 Cut out 4 circular raspberry
mousses using the smaller of the
pastry cutters used to cut the
chocolate sheeting. Sandwich these
mousse cylinders between 2 circles
of dark chocolate sheeting and
place between two of the pools
of chocolate sauce.

"This is disgusting; it's a horrible dish. It's vulgarity pure and simple. It's a dish invented for suburbia; it should be called 'Chocolate Suburbia.'

3 Turn the dark chocolate mousse out of its container and cut in 2, then cut these halves across diagonally to make 4 triangles. Place these on a triangle of dark chocolate as a base and top with a triangle of white chocolate. If necessary, trim the edges to make a clean smooth shape. Place the finished triangles between 2 of the pools of chocolate sauce, with one tip just breaking into one of the pools of sauce.

4 Dust the dark chocolate rings with confectioners' sugar and place them in overlapping pairs in the remaining spaces between pools of sauce, again perhaps just breaking into each pool.

5 Place 2 quenelles of sorbet on top of these rings, one on top of the other at right angles.

6 Garnish the sorbet with the orange zest and some mint leaves. Dust the raspberries with some confectioners' sugar, place them in a decorative cluster on the plate, and top them with the remaining mint leaves.

7 Just before serving, place the chocolate soufflé in the center of the plate.

SERVES 4

ASSIETTE OF CHOCOLATE

Why do we serve it? Because we're commercial. Because, at the end of the day, you have to please the customer. And this does."

VEAL STOCK

Makes about 7 cups

1 lb. veal bones
1 pig's foot, split
2 carrots
1 stick of celery
3 onions
2 lb. veal meat (rib or shoulder
  of veal)
12–16 cups cold water
bouquet garni
oil, for greasing and browning

1 Preheat the oven and a greased
roasting pan to 425 F and brown
the veal bones and pig's foot in
the pan in the oven for about
40 minutes.
2 Wash and peel the vegetables,
then brown them and the meat
in some oil in a deep saucepan
over a moderate to high heat.
3 Add the cold water and bring
to a boil.
4 Add the roasted bones to the
boiling water with the bouquet
garni and allow to simmer for
4 hours.
5 Pass the stock through a
sieve and then let it stand for
10 minutes. Skim the fat from
the top of the stock.
6 Boil the skimmed stock until it
is reduced by half (you will end
up with a *demi-glace)*. Store excess
stock in a screwtop jar in a cool
place or freeze.

CHICKEN STOCK

Makes about 12–16 cups

12–16 cups water
3 lb. chicken wings
2 carrots
1 stick of celery
2 whole leeks
3 onions
bouquet garni

1 Put the cold water in a deep
saucepan with the chicken wings.
2 Bring the water to a boil
and then skim off any fat.
3 Wash and peel the vegetables
and add to the stock with the
bouquet garni.
4 Simmer for 2 hours, then pass
through a sieve. Keep any excess
stock in a covered bowl in the
refrigerator or freeze.

FISH STOCK

Makes about 6 cups

1 piece of bulb fennel, finely sliced
½ cup finely sliced onions
white of 1 leek, sliced
¼ cup butter
2 lb. turbot trimmings (if head
  is used, remove the gills)
4 tbsp. dry white wine
6 cups cold water
3 slices of lemon
3 sprigs of parsley
sprig of tarragon
sprig of cilantro
1 star anise
6 white peppercorns

1 Sweat the vegetables in the
butter over a moderate heat until
they are soft but not browned.
2 Add the fish trimmings and
cook for an additional 1 minute
before adding the wine. Bring
the mixture to a boil and
continue to boil until reduced
by half. Add the cold water and
bring back to a boil again. Skim
off any impurities.
3 Add the lemon slices, herbs,
star anise, and peppercorns
and simmer for an additional
20 minutes. Pass first through a
sieve, then a *chinoise* or conical
strainer. Store excess stock in a
covered bowl in the refrigerator
or freeze.

BASIC RED WINE STOCK

Makes about 4 cups

6 shallots, chopped
3 cloves of garlic, split across
¼ cup clarified butter
3 tbsp. red wine vinegar
3 tbsp. cognac
6 tbsp. port
1 bottle red wine
3 cups veal stock
sprig of tarragon
sprig of parsley
2 tbsp. fresh tomato puree
  (see page 118)

1 Sweat the shallots and garlic in
clarified butter over a gentle heat
until they are caramelized. Deglaze
with the red wine vinegar and
cook until the liquid has almost
all evaporated.
2 Add the cognac and again
reduce until nearly all the liquid
has gone. Add the port and bring
to a boil. Add the red wine and
bring to a boil again. Continue to
boil until reduced by two-thirds.
3 Add the veal stock, tarragon,
parsley, and fresh tomato puree
and bring back to a boil. Simmer
for 30 minutes. Sieve and pass
through a cheesecloth-lined sieve
several times.
4 Store in a covered bowl in the
refrigerator until required. Excess
stock can be frozen successfully.

COURT-BOUILLON

Makes about 7 cups

3 leeks
1 carrot
1 stick of celery
4 shallots
3 onions
1 whole head of garlic
7 cups cold water
1 piece of bulb fennel
sprig of thyme
sprig of tarragon
few stalks of parsley
8 peppercorns
1 tbsp. salt
zest of 1 lemon
1 star anise
1 cup dry white wine

1 Coarsely chop all the vegetables and slice the whole head of garlic across in half to halve each clove. Add just enough cold water to cover (about 7 cups) and bring to a boil. Add the herbs, peppercorns, salt, lemon zest, star anise, and the white wine. Simmer the mixture for 35 minutes.
2 Pass the mixture through a sieve and discard the solids. The court-bouillon is now ready for use. Store any excess in a screwtop jar in a cool place or freeze.

JUS DE NAGE

(COURT-BOUILLON FOR SEAFOOD)

Makes about 7 cups

2 onions
1 leek
2 celery sticks
5 carrots
1 whole head of garlic, sliced across
   to halve each clove
6 slices of lemon
8 white peppercorns, crushed
20 pink peppercorns
1 bay leaf
2 star anise
7 cups cold water
sprig each of parsley, cilantro,
   tarragon, thyme, and chervil
¾ cup dry white wine

1 Coarsely chop all the vegetables and place in a large pan with the garlic, lemon, peppercorns, bay leaf, and anise. Add just enough water to cover (about 7 cups) and bring to a boil.
2 Reduce the heat and allow to simmer for 8 minutes. Add the herbs and cook for another 2 minutes only.
3 Remove the pan from the heat and add the wine. Pour the mixture into a large bowl or jar, cover, and allow to infuse for 1½ days in the refrigerator.
4 Strain the stock through a cheesecloth-lined sieve and discard all the solids. Store the stock in a screwtop jar in a cool place or freeze.

VEGETABLE STOCK

Makes about 3½ cups

2 zucchini
4 onions
1 bulb of fennel
2 leeks
8 cloves of garlic, crushed
14 peppercorns
¼ cup butter
4½ cups cold water
1 cup chopped fresh chervil
1 cup chopped fresh basil
1 cup chopped fresh tarragon

1 Coarsely chop the vegetables then sweat them with the garlic and peppercorns in the butter until they are soft.
2 Add just enough cold water to cover (about 4½ cups) and bring to a boil. Skim and simmer for 15 minutes.
3 Add the herbs and cook for another 2 minutes only. Strain immediately. Keep any excess in a covered bowl in the refrigerator or freeze.

MADEIRA SAUCE

Makes about 5 cups

3 tbsp. oil
1 lb. pie veal
10 shallots, finely sliced
7 oz. mushrooms, sliced
½ head of garlic, sliced across
   to halve each clove
sprig of thyme
¼ bay leaf
10 dried morels
3 tbsp. sherry vinegar
3 tbsp. cognac
3 cups Madeira
3 cups veal stock
1¼ cups chicken stock
¾ cup water

1 Heat the oil in a large skillet over a moderately high heat and sauté the meat for about 10 minutes, turning it occasionally, until it is golden brown all over.
2 Add the shallots, mushrooms, garlic, thyme, bay leaf, and dried morels. Continue to cook for about 5 minutes, stirring frequently, until all the liquid from the mushrooms has gone.
3 Add the vinegar and continue to cook until the liquid has gone—for at least a minute or two to remove all the acidity—then deglaze with cognac, pouring it around the outside of the pan. Pour in the Madeira and cook rapidly to reduce it by about four-fifths.
4 Add the stocks and the water, stir, and bring to a boil. Reduce the heat and simmer for 20 minutes, removing any scum that appears from time to time.
5 Pass the contents three times through a sieve lined with cheesecloth, rinsing the cheesecloth each time.
6 Store in a covered bowl in the refrigerator until required. Excess sauce can be frozen successfully.

FISH VELOUTÉ

(BASIC CREAM SAUCE FOR
FISH DISHES)

Makes about 4¹/₂ cups

10 shallots, finely chopped
2 tbsp. butter
3 cups Noilly Prat
3 cups fish stock (see page 116)
3 cups heavy cream

1 Sweat the shallots in the butter
over a moderate heat until soft but
not browned. Add the Noilly Prat
and continue to cook until the
mixture is syrupy—there should
be almost no liquid left.
2 Add the fish stock and reduce
by half over a high heat. Add the
cream and bring the mixture back
to a boil. Remove from the heat
and leave in a warm place to
infuse for 10 minutes. Sieve the
mixture. Keep excess sauce in a
covered bowl in the refrigerator
or freeze.

JUS DE LANGOUSTINE
OU D'HOMARD

(LANGOUSTINE OR LOBSTER
SAUCE)

Makes about 4¹/₂ cups

5 tbsp. olive oil
48 chopped langoustine heads,
  claws, and body shells
  or
  4 × 1¹/₂ lb. lobster heads
2 tbsp. cognac
¹/₂ stick of celery, diced
¹/₂ small carrot, diced
3 shallots, finely sliced
white of 1 small leek, shredded
¹/₂ head of garlic, sliced across to
  halve each clove
1³/₄ cups dry white wine
4 cups fish stock
  (see page 116)
1¹/₄ cups water
1 star anise
10 pink peppercorns
sprig of thyme
2 large basil leaves
¹/₂ bay leaf
3 tbsp. fresh tomato puree
  (see right)
1 tbsp. tinned tomato paste

1 Heat 4 tbsp. of the oil in a large
skillet and add the langoustine
heads, claws, and body shells
(or lobster heads). Fry them for
about 2 minutes over a moderate
heat, stirring well. Add the cognac
and deglaze the mixture until all
the liquid has evaporated.
2 In a separate large heavy pan,
heat the remaining 1 tbsp. oil and
fry the celery, carrot, shallots, leek,
and garlic until they are soft and
then add the contents of the first
pan to it. Pour in the wine, bring
to a boil, and reduce this by half.
Add the stock and water and bring
the mixture back to a boil, then
add the spices and herbs and the
tomato puree and paste. Bring
this back to a boil and simmer
for 20 minutes.
3 Sieve the contents of the pan
and discard the solids. Then pass
the sauce through a cheesecloth-
lined sieve 5 times, rinsing the
cheesecloth each time. Keep
excess sauce in a covered bowl
and refrigerate or freeze.
Note: you can use up langoustine
or lobster tails in the recipes on
pages 56 and 60.

FRESH TOMATO PUREE

Makes about 2 cups

1 tbsp. oil
1 small onion, finely chopped
3 cloves of garlic, halved but
  unpeeled
sprig of thyme
¹/₂ bay leaf
10 tomatoes, halved and seeded
²/₃ cup dry white wine
sprig of tarragon

1 Preheat the oven to 400 F.
2 Heat the oil in a heavy
ovenproof pan over a moderate
heat and fry the onion, garlic,
thyme, and bay leaf until softened
but not browned.
3 Add the tomatoes and sweat
them for 5 minutes. Finally add
the white wine and the tarragon.
Cover the surface of the mixture
with a round of waxed paper and
cook in the oven until the liquid
has evaporated. Keep excess
puree in a covered bowl in the
refrigerator or freeze.

CLASSIC VINAIGRETTE

Makes about ²/₃ cup

¹/₂ cup olive oil
3 tbsp. white wine vinegar
salt and freshly ground black pepper

1 Beat the ingredients together
and adjust the seasoning. Store in a
screwtop jar until required. Beat
again or shake the jar vigorously
before serving.

CREAM VINAIGRETTE

Makes about ¾ cup

2 tbsp. walnut oil
⅔ cup classic vinaigrette
  (see opposite)
4 tbsp. heavy cream

1 Mix the walnut oil with the classic vinaigrette and then very slowly beat the vinaigrette into the heavy cream. If you desire, add a few chopped truffles. Store in a screwtop jar in the refrigerator for up to 3 days, or freeze if not using immediately.

CLARIFIED BUTTER

1 Take whatever volume of butter you require and melt it in a bowl set over a bain marie.
2 Using a ladle, first remove any scum from the top of the melted butter. Then separate the clear butter on top from the milky residue of impurities on the bottom of the pan.

BASIC PASTA DOUGH

Makes about 2 lb.

4½ cups all-purpose flour
½ tsp. salt
½ tsp. olive oil
4 eggs
6 extra egg yolks

1 Put the flour, salt, and olive oil in a blender and process for a few seconds.
2 Add the eggs and the extra yolks and process until the pasta begins to come together into a loose ball of dough.
3 Knead the pasta dough well on a flat surface, until the mixture is even and smooth.
4 Cut the dough into 8 equal-size pieces and roll them into balls. Wrap each ball in plastic wrap and allow them to rest in the refrigerator for 20 minutes. Any pasta not being used immediately can be frozen.

TAGLIATELLE

Each ball of dough makes one 4 oz. portion

1 Taking one ball of basic pasta dough (see left) at a time, roll the dough out lightly on a floured surface before feeding into the pasta machine. Pass it through the machine several times, until it is the thickness of newspaper. Using the attachment to the pasta machine, cut the pasta into long fine strips of tagliatelle.
2 Cook the tagliatelle in boiling, salted water for 30 seconds. Refresh in cold water and drain thoroughly. Add a few drops of olive oil, toss the pasta to incorporate, and set aside until needed as a garnish.
3 To serve a ball of noodles, simply warm through 4 oz. tagliatelle (one ball of dough) in an emulsion of butter and water. Twist the noodles around a fork, using the other hand, or a serving spoon, as a guide to make the ball.

RAVIOLI

Serves 4 as a starter

1 Roll out one piece of the prepared basic pasta dough (see page 119) gently on a floured surface and then feed it through a pasta machine several times, as for tagliatelle, until it is the thickness of newspaper.
2 Using a pastry cutter, cut out eight 4 inch circles (be careful not to pull the dough as you do this).
3 Spoon a good helping of the filling into the center of each of 4 of these circles. Be careful to leave a good clear edge all around the filling so that the circles of pastry can be sealed together well. Top with the other 4 circles and gently press the edges together. Using scissors, trim any irregular edges of the ravioli. Then gently pinch them all around again to ensure the seal is sound.
4 Bring a large pan of salted water to a boil, drop in the ravioli, and cook for 30 seconds. Refresh immediately in cold water and drain thoroughly. The ravioli can then be kept ready in a covered container in the refrigerator to be reheated before serving.

CHICKEN MOUSSE

Makes about 1 lb.

7 oz. chicken breast (skin and sinews removed), chopped
pinch of mace
1 tbsp. chopped tarragon
1 egg
2 tsp. salt
1 cup heavy cream

1 Process the chicken flesh in a blender for 1 minute with the mace and tarragon.
2 Add the egg and salt and work the mixture for another minute in the blender.
3 Chill the resulting mixture for 10 to 15 minutes in the refrigerator before adding the cream (this will prevent the mixture from separating later).
4 Force the mixture through a sieve to ensure a velvety texture. Taste and adjust the seasoning. Store any excess mousse, wrapped in plastic wrap, in the refrigerator.

CRISPY FRIED LEEKS

Allow per person:

1 leek (white only)
2 tbsp. olive oil
salt

1 Cut the leek white into the thinnest possible matchstick julienne, about 3–4 inches long.
2 Heat the olive oil in a large skillet over a moderate heat and fry the leek until crispy. (Be careful not to have the oil too hot to start with or the leeks will burn.)
3 Remove the leek from the pan and drain on paper towels. Season with salt only before serving.

FETTUCCINE OF VEGETABLES

Serves 4

4 large carrots, washed and peeled
4 zucchini, washed
$1/4$ cup butter
4 tbsp. water
salt and ground white pepper
few drops of lemon juice
6 oz. tagliatelle (see page 119)

1 Cut the carrots into $1/16$ inch × 3 inch strips. Cut the zucchini into strips of the same size, but discard the seedy part in the middle.
2 Blanch the carrot strips in boiling water for 2–3 minutes.
3 In a separate pan, melt the butter with the water and season the mixture with salt and pepper and a little lemon juice. Poach the zucchini strips in this emulsion for about a minute. Add the carrots and the prepared pasta. Simmer for about a minute more to heat through, stirring to mix the carrots, zucchini, and fettuccine thoroughly. Remove them from the emulsion and drain on paper towels.
4 Twist the fettuccine of vegetables and pasta round a large fork, using the other hand, or a serving spoon, to mold it into a ball shape.

ROASTED BUTTON ONIONS

Serves 4

24 button onions
¼ cup butter
salt and ground white pepper

1 Preheat the oven to 425 F.
2 Top and tail the onions and
then blanch them in boiling,
salted water for 3 minutes. Drain
and refresh under cold running
water and then remove the skins
by popping the onions between
the fingers.
3 Melt the butter in a heavy,
flameproof pan over a moderate
heat and add the onions and
seasoning. Sauté the onions for
3 minutes and then cover with a
butter paper. Put the covered pan
in the oven for 5 minutes until the
onions caramelize. Keep warm
until serving.

LENTILLES DU PAYS

Serves 4

1 cup green lentils
sprig of thyme
½ bay leaf
clove of garlic
1 tbsp. butter
brunoise (fine dice) of 1 tsp. each:
   carrot, celery, shallot

1 Put the lentils, thyme, bay leaf,
and garlic in a pan and add just
enough cold water to cover.
Bring to a boil and then simmer
for 25 minutes. Drain the lentils,
remove the herbs and garlic, and
let cool.
2 *To serve:* heat the butter in a
large skillet over a moderate heat
until foaming and then sweat the
brunoise of vegetables until soft.
Add the lentils and cook gently
to warm them through.

POTATO ROSTIS

Serves 4

1 large baking potato
salt and ground white pepper
5 tbsp. clarified butter
   (see page 119)

1 Wash the potato before peeling
and not after, as its starch is needed
to make the rostis stick together.
Peel the potato and grate it on
a mandoline grater into 3 inch
strips of medium thickness.
(It is important that the grater is
not set too thin or the potato will
become too much of a mush.)
2 Wrap the potato in a clean cloth
and squeeze to extract as much
water as possible. Put the potato in
a bowl, season, and stir in 1 tbsp.
clarified butter.
3 Heat the remaining butter in a
large heavy pan over a moderate
heat and place four 4 inch metal
rings in the pan. When the butter
is really hot and foaming, divide
the potato mixture between
the rings.
4 Cook the rostis over a moderate
heat until the undersides are crispy
and honey-colored. Remove the
rings, turn the rostis over, and
cook the other side in the same
way. Drain the cooked rostis on
paper towels and then put them
on a cooling rack to allow air to
circulate around them so that they
stay crisp.
5 *To serve:* warm through in an
oven preheated to 400 F for a
few minutes.

BASIC MASHED POTATO

Serves 4

2¼ lb. russet potatoes
1 tsp. salt
4 cups water
1 cup unsalted butter
6 tbsp. heavy cream

1 Peel and cut the potatoes into
1 inch cubes.
2 Add the salt to the water, bring
to a boil, and poach the potatoes
for 4–5 minutes. Drain and pat dry
with paper towels.
3 Puree the potato in a food
processor and then add the butter
and the cream.
4 Serve while still hot.

CREAMED WATERCRESS

Serves 4

1 cup parsley sprigs
5 cups watercress leaves
6 tbsp. heavy cream

1 First plunge the parsley into a large pan of boiling, salted water and then add the watercress leaves. Continue to boil for 3–4 minutes then drain through a colander.
2 While the parsley and watercress are still hot, squeeze the remaining liquid out of them. (Use rubber gloves to cope with the heat. It is important to do this while the vegetables are hot to retain as much color and flavor as possible.)
3 Place the drained greens in a food processor. Turn on the blender and gradually add the cream as it is running until it is all incorporated. Immediately wrap the puree in plastic wrap to stop oxidization. Keep the puree in the refrigerator until it is needed.
4 When required, heat the puree in a dry saucepan over a gentle heat until it is warmed through. Using a dessertspoon, mold the puree into egg-shaped quenelles to serve.
Note: make creamed parsley in the same way, but using a total of 6 cups parsley instead of watercress.

SPAGHETTI OF CARROTS

Serves 4

4 very large, fat carrots
large piece of butter

1 Trim the ends of the carrots and peel them. Trim the edges of the peeled carrots so that they have the shape of a thick wedge. Then cut the wedges into ⅛ inch slices. Turn the slices so that they are layered on top of one another and cut them again into ⅛ inch strips. The strips should resemble spaghetti.
2 Put the carrot strips in a pan, add enough water to cover generously, and add the butter. Bring to a boil and simmer until the carrot strips are tender but still firm.
3 Drain and serve immediately.

FRICASSEE OF MUSHROOMS

Serves 4

¼ cup butter
2 heaping tsp. finely chopped shallots
8 oz. girolles (or mushrooms in season)
2 tomatoes, peeled, seeded, and finely diced
1 tsp. chopped chives

1 Melt half the butter in a skillet over a low heat and sweat the shallots until soft but not browned.
2 Clean the mushrooms, add them to the shallots, and cook over a moderate heat for 1 minute until the mushroom liquid begins to emerge.
3 Drain the mushroom and shallot mixture through a colander.
4 Return the empty pan to the heat, add the remaining butter, and cook the mushrooms and shallots over a moderate heat for an additional minute.
5 Add the diced tomato and the chopped chives and mix together. Cook for a few seconds until the tomato is warmed through. Serve immediately.

CONFIT OF GARLIC OR SHALLOTS

Serves 4

12 cloves of garlic or whole shallots, unpeeled
sprig of thyme
½ bay leaf
large piece of butter
salt
3 cups rock salt

1 Preheat the oven to 425 F.
2 Wrap the garlic or shallots, along with the thyme, bay leaf, butter, and a large pinch of salt, in foil. Place on a bed of rock salt on a baking sheet in the hot oven.
3 After 20 minutes for the garlic and 30 minutes for the shallots, check to see if they are done. They should be soft (but not mushy) and their skins shiny.
4 *To serve*: remove the garlic or shallots from the foil and top and tail them (but be careful not to remove their skins). They are ready for use as a garnish.

BRUNOISE OF GINGER

1 inch piece fresh ginger root
lemon juice

1 Peel and chop the ginger very
finely. Put it in a pan with just
enough cold water to cover. Add
a squeeze of lemon juice to the
water and then bring it to a boil.
Immediately, drain the ginger and
refresh it in cold water.
2 Repeat this process three times.
(It is necessary to do this because
ginger has such a strong flavor it
could easily overpower that of the
other ingredients of any dish.)
Note: julienne of ginger (very thin
long shreds) is cooked in exactly
the same way.

PUFF PASTRY

Makes about 2¹/₂ lb.

4 cups bread flour, sifted
1 tsp. salt
2 cups unsalted butter, softened
   slightly
³/₄ cup water
2 tsp. white wine vinegar

1 Sift the flour into a circle on a
board. Make a well in the middle
and put into this the salt, ¼ cup
of the butter, the water, and the
vinegar. Mix and knead until the
dough is smooth and elastic. Mold
the dough into a ball and score
with a knife across the top. Cover
the dough with a cloth and allow
to rest in a cool place for about
1 hour.
2 On a lightly floured surface,
roll the dough into a sheet, about
8 inches square, rolling the corners
a little more thinly than the center.
3 Place the remaining butter in
the center of the dough. Bring up
the four corners of dough over the
butter to make an envelope.
4 Roll this out into a rectangle
about 10 X 6 inches and fold in
three. Turn this folded rectangle
by 90°. This constitutes a "turn."
5 Ensuring the rolling pin is at
right angles to the folds, roll out
again to a rectangle the same size
as before and fold in three again
as before. Again turn the pastry
by 90° (in the same direction as
before). Two "turns" have now
been completed.
6 Cover the dough and rest in the
refrigerator for an hour.
7 Roll out again twice into a
rectangle, fold, and turn as in steps
4 and 5. Four "turns" have now
been completed. Rest the dough
again in the refrigerator for
another hour.
8 Repeat stages 4 and 5 yet
again. Six turns have now been
completed. Rest the dough for
one more hour in the refrigerator
and the dough is ready to use.

CRÈME PÂTISSIÈRE
(PASTRY CREAM OR
CONFECTIONERS' CUSTARD)

Makes about 2¹/₂ cups

2¹/₄ cups milk
1 vanilla bean
6 egg yolks
¹/₂ cup superfine sugar
6 tbsp. all-purpose flour
1¹/₂ tbsp. cornstarch

1 Pour the milk into a large pan
and add the vanilla bean. Bring to
a boil and remove from the heat.
2 In a large mixing bowl, beat the
egg yolks and sugar together until
the mixture is pale and thick. Sift
the flour and cornstarch together
and beat into the mixture.
3 Take the vanilla bean out of the
milk and gradually add the hot
milk to the egg, sugar, and flour
mixture, stirring constantly.
4 Return the mixture to the
rinsed-out saucepan and bring
it back to a boil slowly, stirring
all the time. When it has boiled,
reduce the heat to moderate
and cook for about 3 minutes,
stirring constantly.
5 Let the mixture cool: either
put the mixture in a clean bowl
and sprinkle superfine sugar or a
little melted butter on the top to
prevent a skin forming (be sure
to do this if you are going to
store for some time), or pour
the hot mixture on a large clean
marble slab or sheet of parchment
paper which has been sprinkled
with superfine sugar. Stir the
mixture on the slab or paper
until it is cool.

STOCK SYRUP

Makes about 3¹/₂ cups

2 cups superfine sugar
2¹/₂ cups water

1 Dissolve the sugar in the water
by bringing to a boil slowly,
stirring to ensure all the sugar
dissolves. Then continue to boil
the syrup for 1 minute. Sieve, cool,
and store in a screwtop jar in a
cool place.

PÂTE TULIPE

Makes 8/12

½ cup confectioners' sugar
3 tbsp. unsalted butter
1 egg white
6 tbsp. all-purpose flour, sifted
oil, for greasing

1 Mix the confectioners' sugar and the butter together until light and creamy. Add the egg white and then the sifted flour and mix until they form a smooth dough. Wrap the dough in plastic wrap and put in the refrigerator to rest.
2 *To cook*: preheat the oven to 350 F. Using a spoon, spread the dough into 8 circles on a greased baking sheet and cook in the oven for a few minutes until they are golden brown.
3 Press each circle into one of the holes of a tart mold or a muffin pan and then place the same size mold on top of it, pressing down slightly to ensure the tulip shape. Allow to cool, then remove from the molds.
Note: if the mixture cools too quickly during molding, just replace it in the oven for a few minutes to make the mixture soft and pliable again.

TUILE BASKETS

Makes 12

¼ cup unsalted butter
¼ cup superfine sugar
3 tbsp. liquid glucose
½ cup all-purpose flour
oil, for greasing

1 Put the butter and the sugar in a blender and process together until smooth. Add the glucose and flour and blend for another minute. Scrape into a bowl, cover with plastic wrap and allow to rest in the refrigerator for 2 hours to let it firm up.
2 Preheat the oven to 350 F. Roll the mixture into 12 little nuggets in the palm of the hand and place these little balls quite far apart on an oiled baking sheet, to allow for spread during cooking. Press each ball gently into the sheet with the palm of the hand. Cook for 3–5 minutes in the oven.
3 Using a cutter with the same diameter as your tartlet molds or ramekins, cut circles from the tuile mixture. Remove the trimmings and return the circles briefly to the oven to soften them up again. Press the rounds into the molds or ramekins and place an identical mold into it—pressing down gently to ensure a good basket shape.
4 Allow to cool, then remove from the molds once the baskets are firm.

SUGAR CAGE

½ cup superfine sugar
oil, for greasing

1 In a heavy pan, melt the sugar gently and carefully and, when clear, boil it to the hard crack stage (295–320 F)—the mixture should be a golden brown.
2 Plunge the saucepan into ice water to stop the cooking process.
3 Take a spoonful of the mixture and let it drip off the spoon so that it falls into a regular thread. Criss-cross the thread over the back of an oiled ladle to weave a cage or web of sugar. Finish by winding the thread around and around the bottom of the ladle to form the base of the cage. Trim any stray bits of sugar and carefully lift the cage off the ladle and set it down on a cool slab.
Notes: test for hard crack stage by dipping a teaspoon into cold water and then into the syrup and then back into the cold water again. When the resulting cooled sugar ceases to be pliable and cracks like glass, it is ready. Test very frequently as the syrup moves from one stage to the next in a matter of seconds.

It is also a good idea to get everything ready, e.g. an oiled ladle, before you start boiling the syrup.

RASPBERRY COULIS

Makes about ¾ cup

2½ cups fresh raspberries
½ cup superfine sugar
juice of ¼ lemon

1 In a food processor, blend the raspberries and the sugar. Add lemon juice to taste. Pass through a sieve and it is ready to serve. This coulis freezes well.

JULIENNE OF ORANGE ZEST

zest of 1 orange
stock syrup (see page 123) to cover

1 Cut the zest of orange into very thin julienne and blanch briefly in boiling water and then refresh in cold water. Blanch and refresh again.
2 Drain and place in a small pan with just enough stock syrup to cover and bring to a boil. Allow to cool in the syrup.
3 When required, drain off the surplus syrup before serving.
Note: this works equally well with lemon zest or a mixture of both orange and lemon zests.

CANDIED NUTS

Makes about 1 cup

1 cup mixed nuts (hazelnuts, almonds, pine nuts)
1 cup confectioners' sugar
2 tbsp. Grand Marnier

1 Put all the ingredients in a saucepan and stir over a moderate heat. As the contents start to caramelize, scrape the sides of the pan and stir back in the whitish powder to begin crystallization.
2 Continue to stir the contents until completely crystallized. Transfer the nuts to a marble slab or sheet of parchment paper to cool. Store in a screwtop jar in a cool place.

arco
Pierre
White

epilogue

"He was super cool. Steve McQueen in *The Great Escape*, Jim Morrison in the Doors, and Sonny Corleone in *The Godfather*: they were all cool, but MPW was the coolest."

Paul Kitching, Michelin-starred chef, 2004

Ablizzard of frozen white flakes swept across London. Marco, with his small brigade and team of waiters, stared out of the window and across the road to the expanse of Wandsworth Common, now a carpet of snow alight in the darkness. The dining room was empty. Again. Things had not been going well since Harveys opened its doors a few weeks earlier and the brutal winter weather suggested it would be zero takings that night.

Location is everything. Harveys, White concluded, was probably in the wrong one.

Take a stroll along Bellevue Road today and you will be charmed by it. Essentially, it is a parade of shops overlooking the Common. There's a good Victorian pub called The Hope, busy cafés, and little boutiques with cheerful, upbeat names like Tickled Pink. It is a few hundred yards of affluence and friendliness. Back in the late eighties and early nineties Wandsworth was not so wealthy. It had yet to be gentrified, prettied up.

Number 2 Bellevue Road was Harveys. This is where it all began. Revolutions might end in the palace but they are plotted in the workhouse. The British food revolution erupted from here. Or rather, this was the greatest field of victory in the revolution. This is where the chef became The Chef. It was in this restaurant, and through the publication and subsequent extraordinary popularity of *White Heat*,

that the professional cook achieved status. Once it was the lowliest of jobs; now it was one of the most sought after, and by young men and women of all social classes.

On that snowy night Marco stood there with his brigade—Mark and Simple Simon—and Morfudd and her front-of-house team of two, and through the snow they spotted two scarfed-up, sludge-covered people trudging bravely in their wellies and anoraks toward Bellevue Road as if it were the peak of Everest. It turned out to be the governor of Wandsworth Prison, bringing his windswept wife for "a treat." When they had finished their meal Marco joined them for coffee and a chat and was so overwhelmed by their Hannibalesque trek to Harveys that he said, "Don't worry about the bill." They wrapped themselves up again, in that cheerful sort of way the British do before throwing themselves into a snowstorm. Stiff upper lip. Then they stepped out of the restaurant and into the blizzard and vanished.

A couple of months later, in the spring of 1987, the food critic Egon Ronay came for lunch. His review of the restaurant in *The Sunday Times* glowed and gleamed. The phone rang off the hook as the bookings came in. Overnight success was established. Marco White also became Marco Pierre White: Egon Ronay included the middle name in his writeup, and it stuck.

the way

"Number 2 Bellevue Road was Harveys.

This is where it all began. Revolutions might end

in the palace but they are plotted in the workhouse.

The British food revolution erupted from here."

LET'S RETURN to that period, let's go back to Thatcher's late eighties and early nineties, and to that restaurant in Wandsworth, seemingly adrift from the residents of Chelsea, Mayfair, and Knightsbridge because in order to reach it they would have to cross—what horror!—the River Thames. They would have to travel from north London to south London.

But they did, and they came in their Bentleys and Rollers. A couple of months after the snow had melted, Harveys was a destination restaurant attracting gourmets from all over the world.

Harveys was more than theater. It was supposed to be a restaurant but it was an accidental circus. It was a vibrant, overenergized quintessence of nonstop action and insanity, overseen by a lanky, sallow-skinned creature who emerged occasionally from the kitchen into the dining room. Yes, he crossed the divide previously uncrossed by chefs—looking liked he'd crucified himself—and you could eat magnificently as you watched from your seat in the forty-cover restaurant.

Perhaps you'd have guinea fowl, roasted on the bone, skin taken off, legs split, thigh bone taken out, drumstick cleaned up, the whole thing put together, breast carved and laid across the top with jus blonde, joined on the plate by young leeks, roast button onions, and girolle mushrooms on the same plate. Or maybe Pigeon en vessie with a tagliatelle of leeks, or Roast pigeon from Bresse garnished with potato rösti, young turnips, lentilles du pays, and a single raviolo that contained mushrooms, garlic, and thyme. Harveys' dishes were filling and substantial.

They came for the Blanquette of scallops and langoustines with cucumber and ginger; the Feuillantine of sweetbreads; the Hot foie gras, lentils, and sherry vinegar sauce; the Noisettes of lamb en crepinette with fettuccine of vegetables and a tarragon jus. They came for the Hot mango tart; the Passion fruit soufflé; the Lemon tart. At the top of the menu were the words of Oscar Wilde: "To get into the best society nowadays one has either to feed people, amuse people, or shock people—that is all."

"If they could make it into the fourth week they were doing well and those, like Gordon Ramsay, who lasted longer than a year at Harveys were by

The kitchen was small and cramped. Marco put a large table in the center of the room (as Pierre Koffmann had done at La Tante Claire), and he and his chefs worked around it. He had always admired the Box Tree's clever technique of rotating stock (ingredients rather than chicken stock), because it meant they could reduce their waste. Reduced waste equals increased profits. Stock rotation therefore became a rule at Harveys, and this is the way it worked: one day he might do Pigeon with fresh thyme-scented roasting juices and champagne-braised cabbage. If the guests didn't go for it, then he would rethink the dish to avoid binning the pigeons. The next day he might put Pigeon à la Forestière (with wild mushrooms) on the menu and, fingers crossed, that would do the trick. There wasn't enough space for a separate garnish section in the kitchen, so to overcome this, he incorporated vegetables as ingredients served on the plate with the main dish, rather than served on separate side plates.

As the kitchen grew, he used a poky kitchen annex for pastry where two chefs worked, and there were eight in the kitchen. Chefs who came and went on to win Michelin stars included Gordon Ramsay, Phil Howard, Jason Atherton, Richard Neat, Stephen Terry, Anthony Demetre, and Eric Chavot. There was no regimental hierarchy. They all mucked in to do garnish, hot appetizers, main courses, and fish. If there was a table of five, eight cooks worked on five plates, which might mean two people working together on

one dish, then Marco would piece it all together.

So he was the head chef and every other member of the brigade was an "assistant"—there was no sous chef. He told his assistants to call him Marco, rather than Chef. He was still in his twenties and didn't consider himself old enough to be called Chef, although when he gave Kevin Broome, a cook from Manchester, a job at Harveys he started to call Marco "Boss," which others adopted. Thereafter, he was either Marco or Boss until his retirement from the kitchen in 1999. He and his chefs wore blue-and-white striped aprons—traditionally worn by the kitchen commis chefs. "We are all commis, we are all still learning," explained Marco. When you next see a chef wearing a blue-and-white striped apron you will know where this custom began. It is a White legacy, a sort of global salute to the cook from Leeds.

Somehow, he had to find an easy-to-follow way of enabling the brigade to imitate his desired presentation of dishes. He devised a simple method—the plate became a clock. The top of the plate was twelve o'clock and the bottom of the plate was six o'clock; three o'clock was to the right and, of course, nine to the left. So if a chef was dressing pigeon with a petit pain of foie gras Marco could shout across the kitchen, "Foie gras at twelve, confit of garlic at four …" It's foolproof, so long as the cooks can tell the time.

They worked like maniacs, sometimes eighteen hours a day. When Marco wasn't in the kitchen, he would often sit down with pen and paper and draw

and large destined for acclaim."

pictures of dishes that came out of his imagination and which were intended for the following day's menu. Sometimes, in a search of inspiration, he would resort to his trunk, which contained French cookbooks and menus he had collected over the years from other restaurants. Then he might deface the books by drawing his own sketches of dishes straight onto the books' illustrations.

At other times he might pick a main ingredient—sea scallops, lamb, or whatever—and create a long list of other ingredients that would go well with it. He'd study the list, allowing his imagination to go, and then … he would start to see it. With so many of the dishes he would start at the end, if you like, and work his way back, but the process always began with drawing that picture of the plate and what was on it.

White had not a clue about management. Quite simply, it wasn't taught as you worked your way up

the ladder. It was considered that in his kitchen the first three weeks were the toughest period for the new boys. By the end of it they had usually lost weight, gained a dazed expression, and cried themselves dry. That was when the shaking started—and when many of them left. One day they were there, the next they were gone. If they could make it into the fourth week they were doing well and those, like Gordon Ramsay, who lasted longer than a year at Harveys were by and large destined for acclaim. Six of them went on to win Michelin stars of their own.

The kitchen was quiet; there was no chit-chat. Only Marco spoke, and then there were the responses, "Yes, Boss. Two minutes, Boss." If dishes failed to come together on time, Marco would flip. He'd say, "Corner!" and jab a finger toward the corner of the room. The chef would stand in the corner, not with his face to the wall but facing Marco so he could pick up some knowledge while enduring his punishment. One night he sent four chefs to stand in corners and when he shouted "Corner!" at the fifth, the assistant said, "Which one, Marco?" He had run out of corners.

Scorched brioche and incorrectly sliced vegetables were other irritants for the head chef. Marco's premise was this: "In order to achieve my dream I reckoned I needed a brigade with army-standard discipline and, as I had learned at Le Gavroche, discipline is

"When you fear, you question. If you don't fear something, you don't question it in the same way. And if you have fear in the kitchen you'll never take a shortcut."

Marco Pierre White

borne out of fear. When you fear, you question. If you don't fear something, you don't question it in the same way. And if you have fear in the kitchen you'll never take a shortcut. If you don't fear the boss, you'll take shortcuts, you'll turn up late. My brigade had to feel pain, push themselves to the limits, and only then would they know what they were capable of achieving. I was forcing them to make decisions. The ones who left, well, fine, at least they had decided a Michelin-starred kitchen was not for them."

You will be reading this and wondering why on earth chefs worked for him. Why stay with it? There are several reasons: first, all chefs are masochists and many thrive on pain and sleep deprivation; second, they were learning and developing as chefs, becoming more skilled; third, they loved it. There must be those who hated it but, in my years of interviewing chefs who worked with White, I have yet to meet one. Most go out of their way to make a point: "It was tough but I wouldn't change any of it." A bollocking isn't personal. It's a short—sometimes not so short—sharp shock. It's an extremely loud wakeup call. It's smell-the-bloody-espresso time.

Chefs were chucked in the kitchen's large trash can. "In the bin," Marco would say, and a wriggling minion was heaved in the air by his colleagues and tossed onto the waste.

Other times the bollockings included physical abuse. He might severely tug a chef's apron, or grab a chef by the scruff of the neck and administer a ten-second throttle, just to focus him. One night he lifted Lee Bunting and hung him by his apron on some hooks on the wall. The cooks never knew what to

expect from Marco … and neither did he. A film crew arrived for the series "Take Six Cooks" and happened to walk into the kitchen as he was throwing bottles of sauce and oil at an underling. The producer had to duck down to avoid being hit by flying glass. "I don't know if we can film in there," he told the maître d'. "War zones are less dangerous."

During the summer the tiny kitchen, with its glass panel skylights, became blisteringly hot, and Marco and his brigade wore sweat bands on their foreheads and wrists. In fact, Eric Chavot told me of his first day at Harveys, "Marco said to another chef, 'Give Eric a headband.' I wondered what he was talking about. Then he opened a drawer and it was full of headbands and wristbands, and he chucked one at me. I thought, 'Headbands? Wristbands? This is a kitchen, not an athletics track.'"

One day a chef moaned that he was too hot, so Marco took a carving knife in one hand, held his jacket with the other and slashed it. Then he slashed his trousers. Both garments were still on his body at the time. "That should provide a bit of ventilation," he told him, and when he asked if he could change out of his chopped-up clothes, Marco said, "Yes, at the end of the service."

On another day Marco was irritated by the gripes about the heat. "Right, that's it," he said, and turned off the air conditioner. "We'll all roast together," he said.

There was a kitchen porter, Marius, who turned up for work one morning saying he had a sore throat. Someone or other mentioned that the best cure for Marius was Armagnac and Port, so a brandy glass was

"I was forcing them to make decisions. The ones who left, well, fine, at

Marco Pierre White

"Like many of his assistants, Marco survived on Marlboro and caffeine, as well as candy bars. There just wasn't time to eat."

filled with the concoction and he drank it. Half an hour later, when Marius collapsed unconscious on the kitchen floor, they carried him outside to the freezing cold, dumped him in the courtyard, and forgot about him. A snowstorm came and went before someone said in a shocked way, "Marius!" They rushed out to recover his trembling body. Two hours after complaining of a sore throat, Marius was suffering from alcohol poisoning and the onset of hypothermia.

Marius took some time off sick (recovering from the world's worst hangover) and the deputy kitchen porter pitched up. On his first day Marco gave him a few hundred pounds and told him to go to the bookies and put the money on a horse that was racing that afternoon. He left with the cash, muttering the horse's name to himself so as not to forget it. He was never seen again.

PUSH THE SWING DOORS; let's move to front of house. Jean-Christophe Slowik—known as JC— became the maître d' and his job was not just to look after the guests but to hang onto the waiters who were alarmed by the way things worked. The sight that greeted them was one of waiters and chefs suffering chronic fatigue and hunger, all set to the soundtrack of a screaming boss. Even before service started, a new waiter would often make an excuse about getting something from his coat, only to scurry off and never return. These new waiters couldn't work a single hour, let alone an entire shift.

Like many of his assistants, Marco survived on Marlboro and caffeine, as well as candy bars. There just wasn't time to eat. The custom of staff lunches didn't exist, and one day JC explained in his engaging, diplomatic, and charming way that he was having to take money from the petty cash box, nip to the deli a few doors down, and buy sandwiches for his ravenous waiters. He asked, "Is it not odd that we work in a restaurant but have to buy lunch from somewhere else?" From then on, Marco allowed staff to have a meal, but not too often, before service.

Plates returned to the kitchen from the dining room totally clean. For ages Marco thought the customers were so impressed with the food that they were devouring every last speck and drop of jus on the plate. In fact, it was the starving waiters—as they left

least they had decided a Michelin-starred kitchen was not for them."

the dining room and walked along the corridor to the kitchen they would polish off the customers' leftovers, guzzling the remains like famished vultures.

There are stories—myths—that guests were thrown out for asking for salt. Not true. Marco believed that if they wanted salt they could have it. Though customers were evicted if they were rude to the waiting staff or drunkenly obnoxious: "Spoiling the enjoyment for neighboring tables, that's when they were asked to leave," says Marco. There was the "whoosh" technique of getting customers to leave. A squad of waiters would zoom in and, as the offending guests sat there, they cleared the table of everything—plates, glasses, cutlery, wine bottles, you name it—in about fifteen seconds. Only the tablecloth remained. The customers were left sitting there, thinking the table was being cleared for the next course and marveling at the fantastic service. Then JC would swoop in and snatch away the tablecloth. Whoosh! A few minutes earlier the customers were sitting there, drunk and imperious, now they were embarrassed. Humiliated, they'd grab their coats and hurry out onto Bellevue Road. And no, they did not have to pay a bill.

Marco was at the stove in Harveys one night when JC came into the kitchen to say a customer was refusing to pay his bill because he waited twenty minutes for his soufflé. The law of soufflés is that they can take that long. Marco asked JC if the customer's wife had a coat in the cloakroom and he disappeared and then returned saying, "She has a mink, Marco."

"Bring it to me," he said, "and tell the guests to come and see me." The man and his wife arrived at the kitchen where the man said, "Who is the chef?"

"I am."

"You wanted to see me."

"Please stand there," said Marco, telling them to position themselves by a wall. "Wait until I have finished preparing this dish." Husband and wife stood silently for a minute or two, watching while Marco finished sealing or searing, then he turned to them and enquired, "What's the problem?"

The man puffed himself up. "We waited twenty minutes for our soufflé and we're not going to pay our bill now." Marco said, "That's fine. No bill, no mink." He pointed toward an underling in the corner who was holding the coat. The customers looked over. The coat had been kidnapped. Marco said, "No bill, no mink. Make your choice."

His wife perked up, "Pay the bill, darling."

I HAVE KNOWN MARCO since around about the publication of *White Heat*. We worked together on his autobiography, *The Devil in the Kitchen*. I also live

"He reinvented the classics and this was beyond the bravery of most. Somehow he managed to glamorize the shit-storm that happens to produce dishes of such magnitude."

Adam Byatt, chef

"Service was hard but at the end he'd put his arm around you. None of us would change any of it, and of all the chefs I worked for he was the greatest teacher."

Jock Zonfrillo, chef

just across the Common from Bellevue Road. This morning I was passing the restaurant that was once Harveys and for many years has been Chez Bruce, when I bumped into Adam Byatt, another local resident. Adam is chef-patron of Trinity, a fantastic, award-winning restaurant in nearby Clapham that is popular with many Michelin-starred chefs. He told me: "For my 17th birthday my Dad bought me a copy of *White Heat*. Then he drove to Harveys, where he got Marco to sign it for me. I cooked a lot of recipes from that book." In fact, when Adam became a chef his decision to work for Phil Howard at The Square was "partly due to Phil's time cooking with the man himself."

I asked him why Marco and *White Heat* left such a strong impression, and Adam said, "He reinvented the classics and this was beyond the bravery of most. Somehow he managed to glamorize the shit-storm that happens to produce dishes of such magnitude. As a young chef cooped up in a hotel kitchen, *White Heat* was the inspiration I needed to get out, be brave, and make an impact."

These words are familiar to Jock Zonfrillo, the Scottish chef who has made his own spectacular impact on Australia's food-lovers with his restaurant Orana. "I had just turned 15 and was at a hotel in Scotland, and thought, oh my God, I need to be there not here."

By the time Jock made it to White it was a few

years later, and at the Restaurant Marco Pierre White at the Hyde Park Hotel. "I just turned up and knocked on the door. I'd been sacked from my previous job and when I told Marco he said, 'What does your mother think of that?' Marco gave me a job and arranged for me to get accommodation when he found out I was sleeping in the changing room because I had no money. For a period I was addicted to heroin. Marco knew it but it wasn't discussed. Though he was like a father to me, he didn't make me feel like a leper. Service was hard but at the end he'd put his arm around you. None of us would change any of it, and of all the chefs I worked for he was the greatest teacher."

"I owe every bit of success to him," adds Jock. "Marco Pierre White is the Escoffier of our time—there's no question about it."

James Steen
February 2015

Marco Pierre White:
Chronology of a Cook from Leeds

December 11, 1961: Born to Maria Rosa Gallina and Frank White at St. James's Hospital, Leeds, Yorkshire.

February 20, 1968: Death of mother. Marco and his brothers Graham and Clive are raised by father, Frank.

7:30 A.M., March 20, 1978: Aged 16, Marco begins as an apprentice in the kitchens of the Hotel St. George, Harrogate, Yorkshire.

Spring 1979: The two-starred Box Tree, Ilkley, Yorkshire, working for head chef Michael Lawson.

June 24, 1981: Begins work for Albert and Michel Roux's growing empire: first, for a couple of weeks at Le Gamin, London; then at Le Gavroche (two Michelin stars) as demi-chef de partie on Meat/Sauce. Later works (with Mark Bougère) for Albert Roux at his upscale butcher's shop, Boucherie Lamartine, on Ebury Street, in Pimlico, in London.

1983: Chez Nico (two Michelin stars), Battersea, working as cook for chef patron Nico Ladenis.

Summer 1984–January 1985: La Tante Claire (two Michelin stars), working as cook for chef patron Pierre Koffmann.

End of January 1985: Le Manoir aux Quat'Saisons (two Michelin stars) working for chef patron Raymond Blanc.

January 1987: Harveys opens.

marco pie

Spring 1987: Review of Harveys by Egon Ronay in *The Sunday Times*.

July 1987: The awards begin with Newcomer of the Year at The Cateys.

October 1987: Harveys awarded one rosette by the *AA Guide*; one star by the *Egon Ronay Guide*.

December 1987: Newcomer of the Year, *The Times*.

January 1988: Harveys awarded one Michelin star.

Fall 1988: Harveys awarded one rosette (out of three) by the *AA Guide*; one star by the *Egon Ronay Guide*.

January 1989: Harveys awarded one Michelin star.

September 1989: Harveys awarded *The Times* Restaurant of the Year.

January 1990: Harveys awarded two Michelin stars.

Fall 1990: Harveys awarded two rosettes (out of three) by the *AA Guide*; two stars by the *Egon Ronay Guide*.

Fall 1991: Harveys awarded five (out of five) rosettes by the *AA Guide*.

Fall 1992: Harveys awarded three (out of three) stars by the *Egon Ronay Guide*.

1992: Marco awarded Chef of the Year by Egon Ronay.

July 1993: Departs Harveys.

September 1993: Opening of Restaurant Marco Pierre White at The Hyde Park Hotel.

1995: Restaurant Marco Pierre White awarded three Michelin stars; five rosettes by the *AA Guide*; three stars by the *Egon Ronay Guide*; ten (out of ten) in the *Good Food Guide*; 19.5 (out of twenty) and four "chef's toques" in the British edition of the *Guide Gault-Millau*; and Restaurant of the Year by Egon Ronay.

October 1, 1995: First—and only—visit to France, to cook for Rocco Forte's party at Longchamps, in Paris.

September 1997: Opening of The Oak Room at the Meridien Hotel, Piccadilly, transferring three stars from Restaurant Marco Pierre White.

January 1998: The Oak Room retains three stars and is awarded five red knives and forks in the *Michelin Guide*, becoming the first restaurant in Britain to win such an accolade.

December 23, 1999: Final day of kitchen service. At the age of 38, Marco retires from the stove, "returning" his three Michelin stars.

2001: Awarded Chef of the Decade by the *AA Guide*.

rre white

"People say, 'Have you changed?' I am still the introvert. I don't mix. Don't socialize much. The only place in the world where I ever feel comfortable is the kitchen. I still like graft, still like hard work.

When I first walked into kitchens they hadn't changed in thirty years. There were marble tops and wooden benches, and fridges encased in wood. Ovens were speckled enamel. You had your chopping board and you had your knife. There were old-fashioned tiles on the wall. I loved all that. I'm a romantic.

Chefs never rang in sick and weren't late for work. You said, 'Yes, Chef.' You ran, ran, ran … didn't look at your watch. Then it was change. Things went from boil-in-a-bag to cooking à la minute to sous vide. In the old days there was no water bath, no gadgets to make foams. Once upon a time you had to cook. That's why chefs screamed. Then it was like, 'Hey, let's remove the service.'

Once I was the revolutionary. Now I am the dinosaur. I've never sent a fax, don't own a computer, have never sent an email. My mobile phone is a Nokia, twelve years old. I don't understand machinery.

So when they say, 'Have you changed?' I reckon I'm still that boy. I always want to make food taste of food. And I am always intrigued by the story.

A story is way more important than a recipe. A recipe can confuse you but a story … a story can inspire you."

'*White Heat* was the book that made boys want to become great chefs.

Marco is the Mick Jagger of cooking and I am pleased

o have passed on some of my knowledge to him." *Pierre Koffmann, Michelin-starred chef*

"I first came across the *White Heat* cookbook as an 18-year-old, and was completely blown away. The black-and-white pictures by Bob Carlos Clarke sucked me into a world of activity, energy, and relentless passion.

All of a sudden, I recognized the real world of cooking in kitchens in Great Britain. There were no tall white paper hats or polished shoes. Instead, it was blokes with burnt fingers and bags under their eyes, and they looked like they were enjoying a form of trench warfare. Unquestionably, this is the most influential cookbook of all time.

Without Marco Pierre White and the *White Heat* cookbook, many a chef around my age would not be in chef whites. We would probably be on a building site or on a fishing boat.

Stand-out dishes for me were the Sea bass with ratatouille and essence of red peppers, the beautiful simplicity of Escalope of salmon with basil, and the heart and soul of the Piece of Scotch beef with confit of shallots. Fantastic cooking, beautiful photography, all of which has been replicated again and again in kitchens across the country and still, to this day, remains timeless. Young chefs in my kitchen who were not even born when this book was first released still get a huge amount of joy and fire in their bellies from looking at this book.

I will be forever grateful for reading it."

Tom Kerridge, Michelin-starred chef

"Only time will reveal the impact of today's events and seal their relevance in history, and likewise it is only today that we can assess the importance and relevance of the events of years gone by. The timeline of cooking followed a centuries-long and rather dull and meandering path in this country until the seventies. The arrival of a handful of fine French chefs gave it some ripples of, albeit imported, excitement but it is surely fair to say that its direction and all that went on within it was forever changed with the opening of Harveys and the subsequent publishing of *White Heat*. Cooking was brought out from the darkness and the spotlight was shone not only on the wonders that resulted

for diners but on the all-consuming passion that is 'the process of cooking.'

There can be no more an all-consuming passion than cooking and Marco,

with his dynamism and flair, infected a generation of chefs, including me,

with an unprecedented desire to cook wonderful things in a progressive and

artistic fashion. He arrived at a time when able and inspired chefs were few

and far between but the excitement he caused changed the culinary gene

pool forever—thereby sending passionate, high-octane chefs out into the

marketplace to spread the word and change the landscape forever. Music had

The Stones. Cooking had Marco." *Phil Howard, Michelin-starred chef*

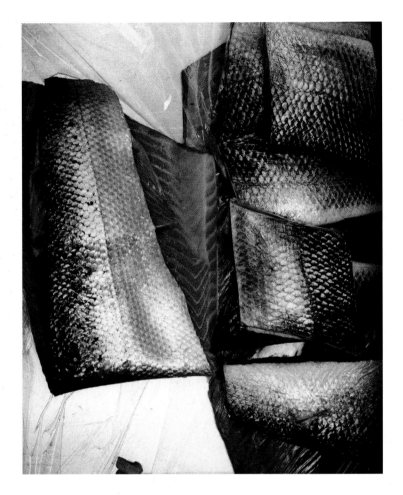

"**_White Heat_ sparked an insane quest for me. It was a quest to be the best chef I could be.**

I found _White Heat_ in a second-hand book shop for four pounds and thought I'd struck gold. There were four copies and I bought all of them. I sold the other three for twelve pounds each. I read mine within two hours, cover to cover.

We all wanted to be a little like Marco. He put chefs in the limelight and he's possibly responsible for the rock-star chef tag.

Occasionally, I pick up the book and flick through it—it's still amazing. Even if you don't like cooking or chefs, it's worth buying for Bob Carlos Clarke's iconic photography."

Sat Bains, Michelin-starred chef

"Marco Pierre White, he's the man who started it. He's the man who put the stake in the ground, gave chefs a profile, put London on the map, as well as shining the spotlight on the gritty side of being a cook; the long hours, the sweaty and small conditions—what actually happened on a kitchen coalface.

I was 19 and I got my arse kicked but I loved every minute of it and learnt a lot. You're getting your arse caned but it was okay because you knew it was making you good. My time at Harveys was instrumental in my career and I will never forget it.

At the time there was no one who could touch him and he'll always be a British institution!

He was a powerful man to play a game of chess with. You can get yourself into check but you can never get checkmate."

Gordon Ramsay OBE, Michelin-starred chef

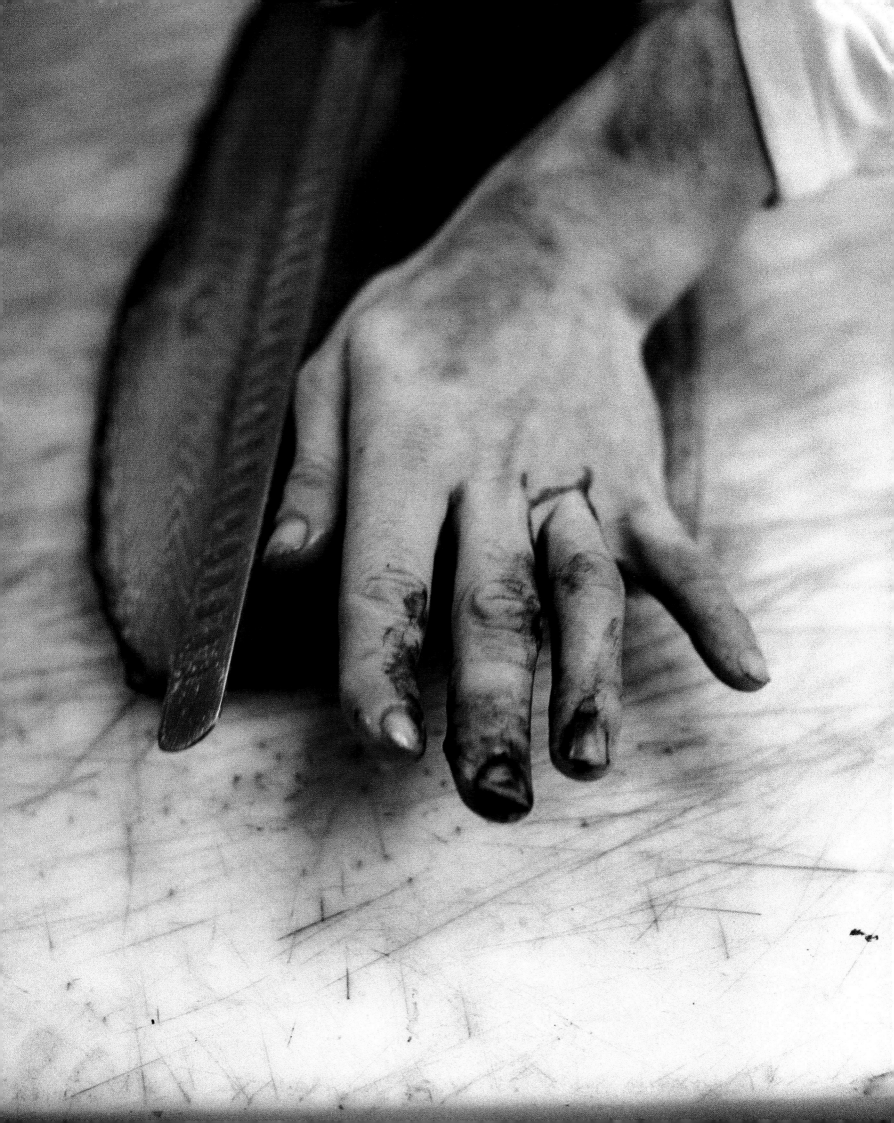

"When I talk to chefs we can all remember the moment when we first laid eyes on the book. It's not that we can all remember—it's that we'll never forget it.

I was just leaving college and had heard the book was coming out. So I went to WHSmith in Sheffield's shopping center. I bought *White Heat* and then, as I walked away from the shop, I opened it up and it was like—FUCK!

You need to know what we had at the time. We had nothing. No one. Cooking was deemed to be done by French chefs; most of them fat, in white uniforms. In France it was considered a prestigious job but in Britain you were just a cook. We had French chefs, of course, like Raymond Blanc and the Roux brothers, but nothing we could really boast about as British.

And then ... I left Smith's and began to look at the book as I walked along. Not only was the food beautiful but here was this good-looking guy with long curly hair, a fag hanging out of his mouth, or half-naked with a shark on his lap. And he was dating supermodels.

As kids, we could have had a dream—the next David Beckham or the next Robbie Williams, let's say. But we'd never achieve it. But all of a sudden, we could say, 'I can do this.' The dream seemed achievable. I mean, for the kid who was a bit of a soccer hooligan with no money and little education … Marco seemed to be sending a message: 'This is a career you can hang on to.' He gave us BELIEF.

I came to London in 1990 and was working for Nico Ladenis, and then I got a job interview with Marco at Harveys in early '93. So I got the long bus journey from Earl's Court to Wandsworth. I weighed about six stone (eighty-four pounds) and was wearing a suit about three sizes too big. And Marco was sat in the bar. He said, 'Hi, I'm Marco.' And I kinda knew that.

I said, 'I'm working for Nico.'

He said, 'Okay. You're hired.'

It was incredible to watch them working in the kitchen—everybody was doing insane hours, and it was almost unsustainable. I was in chef white— that's what I knew: starched whites—and these guys, all of them British, were in Reeboks, black jogging pants, and white T-shirts. When I called Marco 'Chef,' he said, 'I'm not Chef. I'm Marco or Boss.'

Loads of people tried to copy him. They tried to adopt a sort of Marco act. But that's the thing—it was just an act for them. For Marco it wasn't an act, it was the real McCoy. He didn't adopt the bad boy image. He created it. Completely and utterly ripped up the rule book!"

Jason Atherton, Michelin-starred chef

"Wild-haired, madly energized, and brilliantly artistic, Marco put rock 'n' roll into food. He was easily the most gifted young chef of his time, and I am proud to say that this Yorkshireman trained with me at Le Manoir aux Quat'Saisons in the mid-1980s. He was a trailblazer who led a movement against the Establishment chefs, and this had some extremely positive results. Young people looked at Marco as a figurehead and he inspired thousands of today's renowned chefs. There's no doubt that Marco was one of the main chefs to bring about a revival in British gastronomy, and we must never forget that he was the youngest chef ever to win three Michelin stars, at 33. At that age, I had only been cooking for a short while! I salute him."

Raymond Blanc OBE, Michelin-starred chef

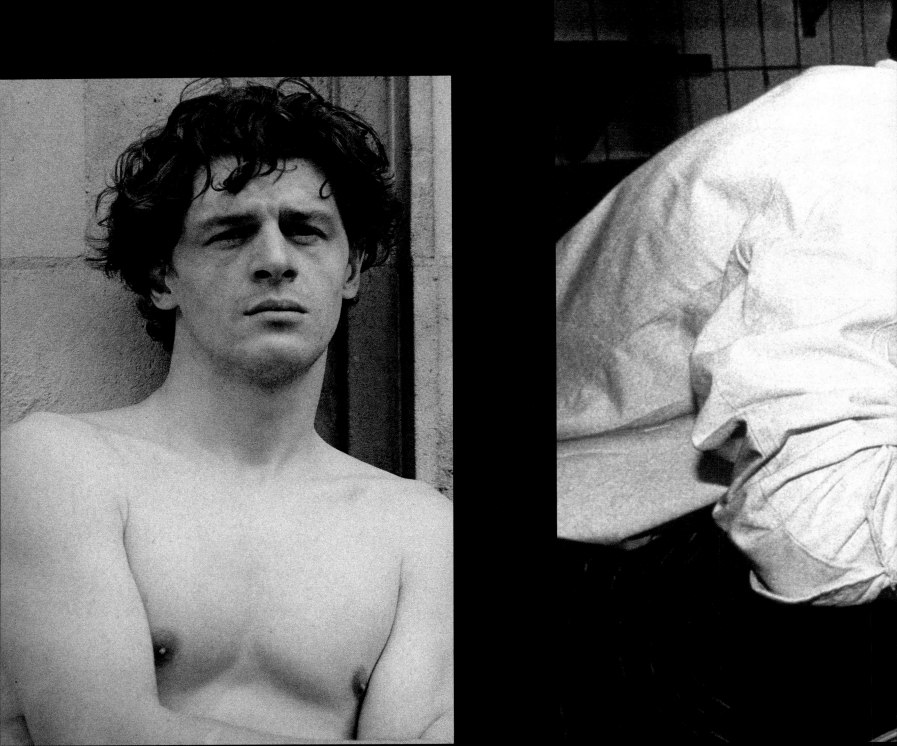

"One day a chef moaned that he

was too hot, so I took a carving

knife in one hand, held his jacket

with the other and slashed it.

Then I slashed his trousers.

Both garments were still on his

body at the time. 'That should

provide a bit of ventilation,'

I told him, and when he asked

if he could change out of his

chopped-up clothes I said,

'Yes, at the end of the service.'"

"Marco took to the kitchen like a hooker to Saint Denis. He was a natural and willing to do it all himself.

His technique was flawless, classic French, his accent was street tough and thuggish.

His physical moves in the kitchen were Nijinsky and his imagination on the plate was pure Stephen Hawking.

He was a savage on the line, and the very first to become famous for treating his team with a humiliating lack of respect.

But it worked in his case. His food was sublime, out of the box, and above all, delicious.

At my young age of 25 (he was 24), he was the toughest and meanest person I had ever worked for and I learned as much about the infinite possibilities of food as I did about how not to treat the team to achieve maximum productivity ... In the end, and after a few years of not talking, I love him like a brother. He is a brilliant artist and deserves all the accolades he ever received, in spades.

White Heat made kitchen work as sexy as being a lead singer and Marco wore it like Mick Jagger.

The book made cooking a legit profession for the young disenfranchised artists looking for a career that paid more than hanging out in front of the Chelsea drugstore with those dudes with colored mohawks."

Mario Batali, Michelin-starred chef

"I don't know if I can adequately convey to you the impact that *White Heat* had on me, on the chefs and cooks around me, on subsequent generations.

Suddenly, there was life pre-Marco, and post-Marco. This book, around which we'd gathered in a prep area, opening it carefully on a cutting board and examining it, changed everything.

It was 1990 in New York City, and none of us knew who Marco Pierre White was. While some of us might have been dimly aware of great chefs in England, that country's restaurant scene was held in little—if any—regard. Our role models, the standard-bearers of excellence in our craft, were generally pudgy French guys, most of them older than us, none of whom we'd ever consider hanging out with. Most of them lived in a foreign land, far away, where they spoke another language and didn't like us very much. Few of them looked fuckable. (Though we were, as it turned out, wrong in this assumption: all those short, paunchy, balding French guys actually got laid like Mötley Crüe.)

We turned the pages with our sweaty fingers, careful not to stain the gorgeous full-color images of classically striking, technically precise, very tasty-looking food. We knew these flavors from culinary school, and from our own experiences with the old-school French, Austrian, and/or German apprenticeship-as-meat-grinder system, a cycle of abuse that passed as learning one's trade back in those days. We could imagine what the food in these pictures tasted like—put the ingredients together in our heads—as so many of them made sense.

But, who was this guy?!

This Marco Pierre White?

The brilliant black-and-white photos by Bob Carlos Clarke confused and inspired us. We all had plenty of cookbooks filled with beautiful photos of artfully arranged food, but we'd never before been able to turn the page and find images of a chef who looked like Marco.

He looked like ... well ... us!

He was skinny like us. We had all learned to despise the idiotic remark, 'Never trust a skinny chef.' All the cooks and chefs we knew looked like starved greyhounds, like workers in a labor camp: ferret-thin, sleep-deprived, undernourished, poisoned by alcohol and nicotine, and God knows what else after work. Fat chefs, to our way of thinking, weren't working hard enough. This guy Marco, he looked like he fucking worked.

And, he didn't look happy, and we loved that, too. All those French guys, depicted in their dining rooms or kitchens, standing with arms crossed, serene, all-knowing, imperious in front of a gleaming array of copper—they looked happy!

None of US were happy! We didn't know any chefs who were happy! We didn't have time to be happy.

What we had time for was work and stress. Marco, unlike any chef we'd ever seen, in any cookbook ever, looked stressed. It was carved into his face. LOOK! He's smoking, leaning up against the KITCHEN WALL, pulling on that cigarette as if he's trying to suck that whole thing down in one go. We knew that feeling. We knew how that cigarette tasted. We were grateful to finally see a chef who admitted to stress and exhaustion like us.

But … but … there was even more.

Once we'd absorbed this long-haired, sweaty, stressed-out, exhausted chef who looked like us and probably had half his more attractive customers bent over a sink in the ladies' room, our colleague who'd brought the book in would draw our attention to the details, the remarkable admissions and assertions in the text.

Three Michelin stars! Awesome. Especially for a guy so close to most of us in age. But then, there, in the first paragraph, after the admonition that if we're looking to read *White Heat* in order to 'cook well' we can 'save [our] money' and pretty much fuck off, is the shocking, bold statement of fact that 'I haven't even been to France yet.'

What??!!

Most of us with any hope of ever becoming a chef, of ever doing the kind of food and having the kind of career that would merit a cookbook, were aimed at the great kitchens of France. That's where you went. (Or at very least you lied about it.)

And if that wasn't enough, there was this absolutely extraordinary passage:

'Any chef who says he does it for love is a liar. At the end of the day it's all about money. I never thought I would ever think like that but I do now. I don't enjoy it. I don't enjoy having to kill myself six days

a week to pay the bank … If you've got no money you can't do anything; you're a prisoner of society. At the end of the day it's just another job. It's all sweat and toil and dirt: it's misery.'

Ten years before my book *Kitchen Confidential* supposedly 'ripped the lid off' the grim realities of the restaurant business, *White Heat* brimmed with casual admissions of what we all knew as chefs: that it was a hard, brutal, repetitive business. That even if we could afford it, we were unlikely to be welcome in our dining rooms. That we were powerless without money. That only by being extraordinary—or at least convincing people that we were extraordinary—could we hope to live like our customers.

White Heat depicted a great chef who was heading straight at that thing we'd all seen: burnout. He knew it. Was conflicted by it. But it wasn't slowing him down. He had somewhere to go and he'd figure it out when he got there.

With *White Heat*, Marco Pierre White gave us all a voice, gave us hope, a new template for survival. We were no longer alone in the world, a despised, underpaid minority, reeking of garlic and salmon. Soon, people would become interested in us. Our customers would actually be curious about our opinions on what they should eat. Eventually, they would want to fuck us—and brag about it to their friends.

This book gave us power.

It all started here."

Anthony Bourdain, chef

"There is no other cookbook like *White Heat*. It deserves all the praise it gets—and my peers in the chef community pretty much all agree it's the best—but I still think it's misunderstood.

Maybe that's because it's not really a cookbook. It's prophecy transcribed, it's the bleeding heart of what it means to be a cook who strives for greatness laid right there on the cutting board, still beating. Nobody before or since has written anything like it. How could they? How else can you only write truth? How can you not lie, not embellish, not play to the audience? I feel like MPW is speaking directly and only to me when I read his proverbs.

The quotes are fucking amazing! This one right here: 'If I came to your house for dinner an hour late, then criticized all your furniture and your wife's haircut and said all your opinions were stupid,

how would you feel? People still come here and expect a three-course meal in an hour. What do they think I do—pull rabbits out of a fucking hat? I'm not a magician.'

The balls it took to strike that tone, that is terrifying—so honest and so direct. In that manner, the book is still unmatched.

He starts with, 'You're not going to see the true Marco until I'm 35 or 40. I haven't even been to France yet. But what's here is me, 1990 vintage, built on a foundation of energy and honesty and quality.' He's basically saying that he doesn't know anything. All he knows how to do is work hard. That all it takes is everything plus no compromising.

I remember looking at *White Heat* before I started cooking professionally and I didn't understand it. The pictures looked scary—Marco Pierre White looked like a scary motherfucker. And he says it: 'I don't try to look like this. It's the kitchen, the wear-and-tear, the stress of the job that makes me look like this.'

How could anyone be so serious about this job—or anything in life? It made no sense. I didn't understand who the chefs he worked for were. I didn't understand the concept. I didn't understand the culinary terms or what life was like in a kitchen. It was just so foreign to me. It was like reading about sex before actually having sex.

Then I became a cook, and it was one of those books I talked about with other cooks—'Ohh! Dude!'—when we drank after work. Everybody wanted to be

MPW, to follow his path.

The photos are so descriptive: they tell you what it's like to be in that kitchen. He's willing to teach and you better listen. (And the message is: if you're not listening, he's going to fucking make you listen.) Look at the kitchen: everything is in its place! Look at his face: he's a fucking scary dude! When you're a cook and you read it, you start to get an idea of what the profession is. You start to understand the terms and the environment and you start looking at this kitchen and what he's trying to do. It plays to that Peter Pan and the Lost Boys mentality of a young cook. He talks about how there's no job in the world as free as being in a kitchen because you get to do whatever the fuck you want.

Then I returned to it as a chef and it was another book entirely. That's part of its magic: it's so short but it's so packed with information, and it's different for everybody who reads it. When I reread it I'm like, 'Fuck! I get it again!' It makes me want to work. It makes me want to strive.

It's so honest. I remember the first time I read Marco on money. He writes, 'Any chef who says he does it for love is a liar. At the end of the day it's all about money. I never thought I would ever think like that but I do now. I don't enjoy it. I don't enjoy having to kill myself six days a week to pay the bank. But if you don't cut the mustard you're finished. If you've got no money you can't do anything; you're a prisoner of society. At the end of the day it's just another job. It's all sweat and toil and dirt: it's misery.'

I didn't understand that as a cook. Maybe I even indulged the idea that he was a sellout. Then I became the chef of my own kitchen, where I had the 'freedom' to do what I wanted and cook what I wanted. But of course that wasn't true. Of course I had to pay the bills. Of course MPW was right. It just took me a long time to understand the lessons.

Every sentence in the book is like that, a nugget of truth that's waiting to be unearthed and understood, ideas that reveal themselves with time. *White Heat* has all the wisdom it takes to be the best packed into one slim volume, written by a guy who hadn't even gone to France yet. It's so humbling and so amazing. It's the best cookbook ever written, and it's so much more than that, too."

David Chang, Michelin-starred chef

White Heat

Early in 1986 Bob and I met Marco. He came to tea with a female friend of ours. He was tall and skinny with wild tousled hair, extremely charismatic. He spoke with such intensity and passion about his food, he talked of bladders full of stuffing exploding on your plate and pig's feet filled with truffles.

He was desperate to cook for us and told us all about his new restaurant, Harveys, in Wandsworth. Later that night Bob said to me, "Well, he's either completely mad or he's a genius!"

They had a great similarity, they were both passionate about what they did and perfectionists. The combination of Marco's cooking and Bob's photography was dynamic.

Bob rarely took pictures of men but thought Marco would look great lying on a tombstone, very romantic and Pre-Raphaelite. Bob nicknamed Marco "Byron of the Backburner;" the first pictures of Marco were shot in a dark moody cemetery in Bethnal Green.

We were frequent guests at Harveys and Marco would book us a late table so he could join us after service. Marco would appear out of the kitchen worn, tired, thin, and exhausted. His first question was always about the food—it was a huge learning curve for Bob and I as we had never been exposed to cooking on this level.

One evening Marco confessed that he had been sleeping under table nine as he was too tired to go home.

"Sleeping Under Table Nine" was the first working title for the book!

"White Heat" was a title that came to me about four o'clock one morning; it now seems obvious but not twenty-five years ago.

Some time later Marco appeared on our doorstep and told us he had been approached by a publisher to do a cookbook. He asked Bob if he would do the pictures. Bob was honored but said that he was not a food photographer and perhaps he should do some test pictures.

He packed his cameras and lights and went up to Harveys at about nine o'clock one evening. He arrived home at two o'clock looking shattered but on an adrenaline high.

"It was amazing and terrifying," he said, "like a war zone. I know I can shoot this book. All black and white, the speed, the noise, the shouting, the passion, the anger. I can see it now: Marco in the heart of the kitchen. I know how I am going to shoot this book, like Don McCullin, except I'm in a kitchen.

A few days later he showed the first pictures to Marco and explained his idea for the war in the kitchen and the calm of the restaurant. Several nights later at about 2.30 in the morning, Bob and I were woken by banging on our front door. It was Marco, straight from the restaurant with a bucket of mussels in one hand and a pile of tablecloths in the other. Marco had understood Bob's vision and had scribbled more ideas on the tablecloths.

Bob and Marco spread the cloths on the floor and started to discuss the final ideas for the book. The big sticking point was the food and Bob was not convinced he could do it justice. He had decided to

"'It was amazing and terrifying,' he said, 'like a war zone. I know I can shoot this book. All black and white, the speed, the noise, the shouting, the passion, the anger. I can see it now: Marco in the heart of the kitchen.'"

use Polapan film, amazing 35mm film that you could develop in a box immediately. It had an incredible quality and you could see the pictures instantly, but the film was fragile and would damage and scratch, and this became part of the quality of the photographs.

Agonizing nights Bob spent in Marco's kitchen sometimes coming home at 2 and 3 A.M. without any really different pictures and then suddenly lots would happen in one night. In all he shot over 3,000 photographs, many of which were too damaged to use.

Obviously both Marco and Bob had all sorts of other work commitments and shortly before it was finished they both seemed to want to give up. Marco had fired several book designers including his own restaurant designer who he apparently threw out of a window.

I sat with Marco and Bob as they talked, they seemed flat and exhausted. I think they were too close to it.

I finally said, "Whatever you feel, this book is nearly there. Don't give up now it's nearly finished.

The pictures and the words and the food are amazing. It's going to change the world of cookbooks forever!"

They both just stared at me and said, "Okay."

And although I don't think I had any real insight into what was about to happen, it did change the world of cookbooks. No one had ever taken photographs of a real kitchen working on that high adrenaline buzz and certainly not published them in a book. It inspired a generation.

Some months after the book was published, Bob was approached by several publishers and their new up-and-coming chefs as they all wanted to be photographed like Marco. Bob said he could never replicate what he had done with Marco because there was no one else like him. He was unique.

Many of the pictures were deemed unsuitable, the publishers were frightened. It is great to see that twenty-five years on we finally get to see the complete set. I think Bob would be extremely pleased.

Lindsey Carlos Clarke
February 2015

Bob and I met in 1986. We were introduced by a girlfriend of mine, whose name was (and still is) Lowri-Ann Richards, LA for short.

Bob and his wife Lindsey invited LA and me for tea. It was an encounter that has remained in my memory because, as we sat at the table in the Clarkes' home in Fulham, I felt myself under the constant gaze of Bob. He just stared at me. I left muttering to LA, "He's a bit peculiar."

The following day, LA phoned to say, "Bob was mesmerized." She said he wanted to photograph me, and not just a head-and-shoulders portrait shot. We went to a cemetery in the East End, I stripped to the waist, lay on a tombstone, and he took some photos. Done. Then I went back to the kitchen to cook for my guests.

The concept for *White Heat* came about a couple of years later, when I was approached by publishers to write a cookbook. I thought Bob would be the perfect partner, even though he was an established fashion photographer and so food was not his genre. In fact, Bob was an immensely intelligent, highly visual man.

I arrived at his house with a pile of linen tablecloths—he must have thought I was on my way to drop off the laundry. The tablecloths contained the concept for what would become *White Heat*—over the linen I had drawn pictures of my dishes and mapped out my own vision for the book. I knew I wanted it to be different. There had to be lots of big black-and-white photos. Bob, the natural observer, could see where this was heading. The project excited him. He came on board, and how lucky was I! Bob, or maybe it was Lindsey, came up with the title.

It is not as if we set out to create an iconic cookbook, and did not realize the impact it would have. Bob, meanwhile, was inspired by Don McCullin's photographs of the Vietnam War. A professional kitchen, of course, is not a ghastly war zone but you can see where Bob was coming from.

My life in the kitchen is like a blur. It's like a dream. I did not consider myself an ambitious person, but was driven by an addiction—pure and simple—to adrenaline.

In *White Heat* there's that massive quote of mine which reads, "I can't work in a domestic kitchen; it's just too confined. There's no freedom and there's no buzz. At home I'm not hit with forty covers in half an hour, so there's no real excitement." It may have explained why I was rarely at home, let alone in the kitchen at home. Things change. These days I love to cook at home. Cooking for family and friends is one of my great pleasures—simple roasts and one-pot dishes that can be plonked in the middle of the table.

To this day I frequently come across people who say one of two things to me.

Either: "The first proper restaurant I went to was Harveys. My father/uncle/godfather took me."

Or: "The best meal I ever ate was at Harveys."

These are the finest compliments a chef can receive, and I am forever indebted to my team—and I include the kitchen porters because they never get any praise.

So what came later? Bob was one of those friends who pops in and out of your life, rather than being a constant presence. Six months might pass before we saw each other, but when we spoke we could pick up where we had left off.

Shortly before his death, which was a few weeks before publication of my autobiography, we had seen quite a bit of each other and enjoyed a good lunch. Then I got a call to say that he had died.

The *White Heat* of 1990 contains its own dedication.

This special edition of *White Heat* is dedicated to Mirabelle and Rose.

Marco Pierre White
February 2015

index of recipes

Assiette of chocolate 114

Basic mashed potato 121

Basic pasta dough 119

Basic red wine stock 116

Biscuit glacé 100

Blanquette of scallops and langoustines with cucumber and ginger 62

Braised pig's trotter 'Pierre Koffmann' 84

Brunoise of ginger 123

Chicken mousse 120

Chicken stock 116

Clarified butter 119

Classic vinaigrette 118

Confit of garlic or shallots 122

Court-bouillon 117

Cream vinaigrette 119

Creamed watercress 122

Crème pâtissière 123

Crispy fried leeks 120

Escalope of salmon with basil 72

Fettuccine of vegetables 120

Feuillantine of sweetbreads 64

Feuilleté of roast rabbit, spring vegetables, jus of coriander 68

Fillet of sea bass with ratatouille and an essence of red peppers 74

Fish stock 116

Fish velouté 118

Fresh tomato purée 118

Fricassee of mushrooms 122

Fricassee of sea scallops and calamares with ginger, sauce nero 70

Gratin of red fruits 102

Grenadine of veal, creamed watercress, spaghetti of carrots, fricassee of girolles 89

Hot foie gras, lentilles du pays, sherry vinegar sauce 67

Hot mango tart 104

Julienne of orange zest 125

Jus de langoustine ou d'homard 118

Jus de nage 117

Lemon tart 106

Lentilles du pays 121

Lobster with its own vinaigrette 78

Madeira sauce 117

Nage of sole and langoustine with carrot 77

Navarin of fish 76

Noisettes of lamb en crepinette, fettuccine of vegetables, jus of tarragon 94

Passion fruit soufflés 107

Pâte tulipe 124

Peach melba 110

Piece of Scotch beef, confit of shallots and garlic with a red wine and shallot sauce 98

Pigeon en vessie with a tagliatelle of leeks and truffles, jus of thyme 96

Potage of shellfish with truffle and leek 61

Potato rostis 121

Puff pastry 123

Raspberry coulis 124

Ravioli 120

Ravioli of lobster with a beurre soy sauce 56

Red mullet with citrus fruits 82

Roast button onions 121

Roast guinea fowl with wild mushrooms 92

Roast pears with honey ice-cream 108

Roast pigeon from Bresse with a ravioli of wild mushrooms and a fumet of truffles 86

Salad of red mullet, sauce gazpacho 66

Savarin of raspberries 112

Spaghetti of carrots 122

Stock syrup 123

Sugar cage 124

Sugared nuts 125

Tagliatelle 119

Tagliatelle of oysters with caviar 58

Terrine of leeks and langoustines, water vinaigrette 60

Tranche of calves' liver with a sauce of lime 90

Tuile baskets 124

Turbot with baby leeks, a ravioli of scallops, choucroute of celery with a grain mustard sauce 80

Veal stock 116

Vegetable stock 117

Woodcock, lentilles du pays, with a red wine sauce 88

and acknowledgments

The photographs in *White Heat* were taken with an Olympus Ti using Polaroid Polapan and Polagraph 35mm black and white film.

Dupe color transparencies by T&S Labs Ltd.

Photography production and title by Lindsey Carlos Clarke.

Bob Carlos Clarke would like to thank Polaroid, Olympus and T&S Labs for their kind support.

25th anniversary edition

A special thanks to James Steen for writing the epilogue and to all those who shared their memories of Marco and *White Heat*: Jason Atherton, Sat Bains, Mario Batali, Raymond Blanc OBE, Anthony Bourdain, Adam Byatt, David Chang, Phil Howard, Tom Kerridge, Paul Kitching, Pierre Koffmann, Gordon Ramsay OBE, and Jock Zonfrillo.

With thanks to Lindsey and Scarlett Carlos Clarke, Pat White, Ghislain Pascal, The Little Black Gallery, Chau Digital, and Olympus.

Find out more about Bob Carlos Clarke by visiting www.bobcarlosclarke.com

And for Bob Carlos Clarke print sales contact www.thelittleblackgallery.com